A pure gesture of generosity from Dr. Steven Hryszczuk to the world! After creating his own dream life with his family, Steve shares all his success secrets, making what he did imminently doable for anyone open to catching "the newest wave of entrepreneurship." From letting go of "time poverty" to giving up his addiction to peer approval, Steve lays out the strategies and mind shifts required to succeed in an often misunderstood business model. If you are looking for true abundance of time and money, let Steve be your guide to Royalty Income.

–DR. JOSEPHINE GROSS,
Editorial Director, Networking Times

In *Royalty Income*, Dr Hryszczuk shares invaluable insights on how to earn while you sleep and avoid the trap of trading hours for dollars. He is a role model and mentor who practices what he teaches."

–DENIS WAITLEY,
author of *The Psychology of Winning*

Many dream of an income stream but acting with discipline and determination to achieve it is something else entirely. Dr. Steve Hryszczuk shines an exciting laser beam of clarity onto the path and inspires you for success. *Royalty Income* can transform the lives of all wishing to replace the drudgery of a job or a profession with the passion of the entrepreneur.

–RABBI DANIEL LAPIN,
author of *Thou Shall Prosper*

ROYALTY INCOME

ROYALTY INCOME

The Business of Getting Paid More Than Once

STEVEN W.
HRYSZCZUK, DO

Royalty Income

Published in the United States by Credo House Publishers,
a division of Credo Communications, LLC, Grand Rapids, Michigan
www.credohousepublishers.com

ISBN: 978-1-625860-33-0

Interior design by Sharon VanLoozenoord
Editing by Joy Golson

Printed in the United States of America

First edition

Table of Contents

"I dedicate this book to
King Jesus, the Lamb of God,
the author and perfecter
of our faith."

Preface

IN 2007, I FELT TRAPPED. I was practically living in the hospital. As a partner in a busy anesthesiology practice, some weeks I was hardly at home. I missed my four kids. I knew I would have regrets if I didn't make some changes. I hate regrets. My children were growing up fast, and I was missing out. *They* were missing out.

I prayed for a solution. *How can I provide financially without selling all of my time for money?* A friend shared some business concepts with me that I had never heard of. At first I resisted, but eventually they made sense. Today, I work at the hospital only when I choose to. I am financially independent.

In 2010, at the age of 43, I left my full-time medical practice because of a significant recurring income stream from a business in an industry called *network marketing.* It is now my privilege to show others how to do the same thing.

Introduction

Royalty income *(also called* residual, passive,
or recurring income*) is income that continues to be generated after the initial effort that created it has stopped.*

DO YOU FEEL LIKE you're working really hard but not getting ahead? Do you ever feel like you spend too much time at work? Are there important things you'd like to do, but you just never have enough time? That was me, just a few years ago.

Now my situation has changed. Completely. I had no business or financial training, and yet I was able to build a strong business in an industry that most people either don't know about, or they think it's not for them. I know that plenty of people could do what I've done, if only they understood how it works. This book is my attempt to give you a fresh look at the newest wave of entrepreneurship: network marketing.

If you'd like to enjoy a *continual* stream of recurring income without having to "go to work everyday," you will need to educate yourself on business fundamentals and learn new skills. If you'd like a *significant* stream of recurring income, you must be willing to teach these concepts to others. If you're the kind of person who finds something good and keeps it to yourself, this business is probably not for you.

I will show you how to create massive value for the marketplace, and how this almost magical thing called royalty income can occur as a result. I will shed light on a poorly understood business model that best-selling author and economist Paul Pilzer calls "the perfect storm of unprecedented economic opportunity." Many otherwise-bright people are in the dark when it comes to the latest advancement in business marketing.

It's unfortunate that most people don't know there is a low-risk way to grow a profitable business. The dream of entrepreneurship is still available for all takers. I believe that network marketing is the best way for the average person to build a royalty income business. I'll show you how to do it part-time *and* without losing friends.

You have no prior business experience? Neither did I. No formal business education? Me neither. You don't like selling? I'm with you. If you want more and are ready to learn, then network marketing could be your vehicle to a better financial future.

Why am I qualified to explain this to you?

Because:

1. I earned over $1 million in commission in my first six years.
2. I mentored a business partner who has earned over $2 million.
3. I'm an average person who earns an annual, multiple six-figure *residual* income with zero to ten hours of work each week.
4. I love to teach. I derive great satisfaction from seeing people "get it."
5. I worked really hard to figure this business out. In my experience, that gives me an advantage in explaining it to you. When something comes easy for a person, they often have a harder time teaching it to someone else who is struggling. Have you ever noticed that?

I've had the privilege of mentoring many others in this business. Some have gone on to build businesses bigger than mine. I've been blessed to live my dreams, and I want to help you live yours.

A few caveats:

This is not a get-rich-quick project. It will require the best of you. In order to offer value to the marketplace, you must first develop skills. This will take lots of work. You must be willing to give consistent, part-time effort for the next three to five years developing new skills.

If you prefer to take the path of least resistance, these ideas are probably not for you. If you're the kind of person who enjoys the reward of reaching the mountaintop, read on.

The financial and business concepts I'll show you may challenge your beliefs about what you think is possible. If you keep an open mind, you will see what most others don't see. Discovering a way to make someone's life better is how we add value the marketplace, and it's the essence of entrepreneurship.

All that to say, it's God's grace in my life that gives me purpose, and helps me remain faithful at what I'm called to do. He has been over-the-top generous with me, and it would be selfish for me to not share this good thing with you.

> "Our goal should not simply be to do work, but to increase the human race's capacity to cultivate the created world. It is a worthy goal to want to make a contribution to your discipline, if possible; to show a better, deeper, fairer, more skillful, more ennobling way of doing what you do."
>
> —Timothy Keller, *Every Good Endeavor*

CHAPTER 1
What Is Royalty Income?

WHEN I WAS A KID, we rarely discussed financial or business concepts. I heard the adage that "money doesn't grow on trees," but that was about it. I didn't take business classes in college. So for me to build a business that made me financially independent at 43 years of age is remarkable. What's even more remarkable is that I launched this business in 2008, during one of the worst economic downturns in recent history.

Get this: The business grew without having any employees, no payroll, no inventory, no building lease, and no costly legal expenses. My main expenses were a computer and a cell phone, which I already had.

The story I want to tell you is how it happened. If you understand how the business works, there's a good possibility that you could do it, too. Unfortunately, the business model I found is poorly understood, and there is plenty of misinformation and confusion out there about it. Many people *think* they know how it works, and in turn, disparage it. Others think they know how it works, and don't believe *they* could do it. Either way, both groups lose.

Let me ask you a question—When you were in high school, if you had seen an elective offered called *MONEY 101: Learn How to Get Paid More Than Once for Your Work,* would you have taken that course?

Would you be curious, maybe even skeptical? How to get paid *more than once*? Who gets paid multiple times for working *once*? It seems too good to be true. This must be some sort of scheme. Everyone knows you get paid only ONCE for working. These would have been some of my thoughts; maybe they would be your thoughts, too. That's okay, just keep an open mind.

Let's define a couple terms. There are two primary kinds of income: *linear income* and *royalty income.* The term "linear income" refers to getting paid *one time* for your work. You work eight hours and you get paid for eight hours. Once. You work a 40-hour week, you earn 40 hours' worth of pay. One time. This is what most of us are familiar with. It's what seems logical and realistic to us. It makes sense.

Hang on to your seats. There's another kind of income called "royalty income." With royalty income, you could work eight hours, and get paid for 80 hours, or 800 hours. No joke.

As I write this, my family is living in Honduras. I'm an anesthesiologist at hospital Loma de Luz. My wife Andrea is teaching first-graders at El Camino, a bilingual school. Neither of us get paid to work here. Yet every week, we have a sizable check deposited into our bank account that takes care of our financial needs. And that check is not from the hospital or school. The check comes from our royalty income business. Pretty amazing.

Sound too good to be true? Well, it *is* that good. And it is true. So, unless you were born yesterday, you should be wondering, *What's the catch*? Excellent question. We all know that you don't just show up, work for eight hours, and then pocket 80 hours of pay. Right? You're right. There *is* a catch.

Here it is: In order to earn a royalty income, you must *work for free* in the beginning.

Working for Free

You heard me right. Work for free. As in, put in lots of hours' worth of work, only to bring in zero income? *That* kind of free? Yep. Who can afford to work for free like *that*? Well, I said that royalty income is possible; I *didn't* say it was easy. Here's an example of working for free.

Years after John Lennon's death, his estate still earns millions of dollars in income, *royalty* income. How does this happen? Well, think back to when young John was first learning to play guitar and sing. Did he get paid a lot back then? Not likely. He actually had to buy a guitar, probably even pay for lessons. In that sense, for many years, John Lennon "worked for free."

As an adult, John began to earn serious money with his music. Even decades after his death, people still buy his work, and his estate still earns big money. This phenomenon is most commonly known as royalty income. Musicians, authors, movie producers and oil well owners also earn royalty income.

There are many names for this type of income that continues to come in after the initial work that created it has stopped. Names like residual income, continuous cash flow, passive income, annuity income, and interest income are a few other ways to describe it. All of these terms describe ways of getting paid repeatedly for a one-time effort.

Admittedly, John Lennon is a unique case. Not many of us are capable of becoming musicians, novelists and artists whose ongoing sales will continue to bring in income. In contrast, the business I will describe for you is accessible to almost anyone.

Yes, there certainly *is* a catch. The catch is that you must first provide a service or product for the marketplace, even if it means you don't *initially* get paid to do it. This is what businesses do. Who can do this? Almost anyone can.

One downside of starting a traditional business (with a linear income model) is that it usually requires putting lots of capital at risk. It's an all-or-nothing proposition. Many new business owners pursue investors, crowdfunding, bank loans, take out a second mortgage on their home—whatever they can do—and the financial stakes are high. If the new venture doesn't create cashflow quickly enough, the entrepreneur may run out of capital before the business becomes profitable. The harsh reality is that most new businesses don't survive the first five years.

In contrast, the business I'll show you requires comparatively minimal financial risk, and you can grow it part-time. The financial stress of carrying tens or hundreds of thousands of dollars of debt will not be a factor here.

To earn a royalty income, you first select some type of service or product to offer people that they will want to buy again and again. Think of switching on the electricity or pumping gas in your car. You keep buying certain things over and over because you need them every day. This idea of repeat sales is the foundation of a royalty income.

While most of us will never own an oil well nor a power plant, there are other ways to grow a distribution network of high demand products that require repeat purchases to enjoy.

Distribution Networks

Distribution networks are all around us. The more obvious ones are high power lines and gas stations. Creating fuel and power networks costs millions of dollars. In contrast, the network I own is almost virtual. Millions of dollars' worth of products are continually flowing to customers, but you can't see the transactions with your eyes. This business is real, but it's not conventional. I can't point to it and show you and say, "there it is."

With my business, a company makes and distributes a high-quality, high-demand product. The company receives the orders and collects the payment. The company organizes the distribution process of physically getting the products to the consumer's doorstep with whatever shipping method the customer wants. It can be one-day shipping, or take five days. Whatever the customer wants.

That's a lot of moving parts. And get this: I am not a part of any of the actual physical distribution process. It's not my concern. The company even offers a money-back guarantee to my customers. The company handles all of this! That's why I call it a *virtual distribution network*. It's practically virtual from my perspective.

So what *is* my role in the whole process? I find the customers and answer their questions. More on that later.

Imagine trying to roll a big, heavy tire. It takes lots of effort in the beginning to get it moving. But once the tire starts to roll, it takes very little effort to *keep* it going. The big tire just needs a small tap every once in a while to keep going. The hard work has already been done. Now that the big tire has been set in motion, it rolls and rolls and rolls with little effort. A well-known saying for those who enjoy residual income is "overworked and underpaid in the beginning, and underworked and overpaid in the end."

Here's the good news: A royalty-income business can be launched and maintained with as little as five to ten hours of work each week. You work at it whenever you choose to carve out the time. Total flexibility. You do this while you keep your full-time job. If a better future for yourself and your family is not worth carving out ten hours a week, then this business is not for you.

Is a royalty income realistic for the average person?

An initial question to ask is: *A*re you willing to step outside your comfort zone? I'm comfortable putting people to sleep in the operating room. I'm comfortable treating their pain. I'm comfortable waking them up when the surgery is done. This is what I know; it's what I'm comfortable doing.

But when I began my business, I did not feel comfortable asking people whether they used nutritional products. I wasn't comfortable when someone was a no-show to a business meeting. I wasn't comfortable when someone asked me a question I couldn't answer. I wasn't comfortable with any of that.

See what I mean? Can you voluntarily accept feeling uncomfortable while you learn something new? This is very hard for most of us. We always want to look good. And it's hard to look good when you're learning something new. Are you willing to feel uncomfortable while you learn something new? If you can answer that question affirmatively, then a royalty income business is realistic for you.

The next question to ask yourself is: what kind of financial intelligence do you have?

How we think about money

There are various ways that people think about making money. I am indebted to Robert Kiyosaki's work in *Cash Flow Quadrant* here. His books have been invaluable for me as I have learned to think differently about money.

For most of us, we are comfortable having a job. This is what we see most people doing—having a job and getting paid every week or two. We learn to accept this as safe, as normal, even as the responsible thing to do.

Having a steady job with a linear income characterizes what Robert Kiyosaki calls the "E Quadrant" for employees. These are the people who feel most comfortable when they have set hours, a boss, and a regular paycheck. For E Quadrant people, the idea of "working for free" (even part-time) might be unacceptable. They have perhaps never thought about delayed financial gratification.

If the E Quadrant is where you are currently, recognize that is not inherently good or bad, just descriptive. It describes your personal relationship with making money. But be honest with yourself about *why* you are in E, and whether you *want to stay* there. Self-awareness is where we begin. The beautiful thing is, you don't have to stay in your current quadrant unless *you choose* to stay.

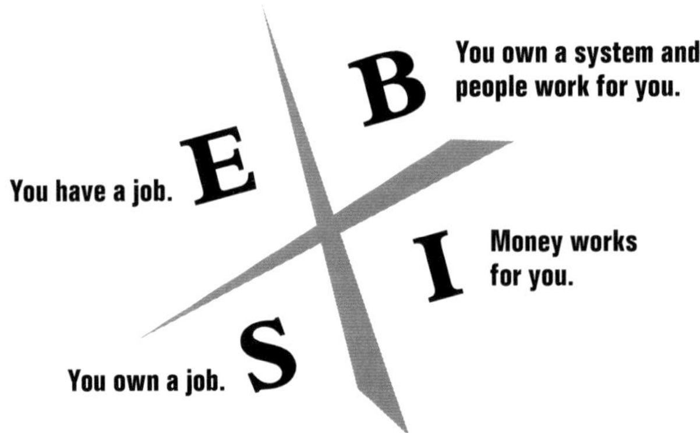

The next group is what Kiyosaki calls "S Quadrant" people. S stands for self-employed. This category characterizes people who are generally ambitious and hardworking. These are rugged individualists who offer the marketplace their skills. They are shopkeepers, consultants of all sorts, professionals, and independent contractors. Self-employment can be a very rewarding way to work, but also exhausting. Self-employed business owners can work harder than anyone else.

As the saying goes, employees have a job; but with self-employed people, the job often has *them*! Self-employed types might create some recurring income, but with extra burdens—like raising capital, making payroll, and managing employees.

If you don't want to sell most of your time for money and earn only linear income, then you must cross over to the right side of the quadrant, to the B and I Quadrants. This is "magical place" where royalty income is found.

The next quadrant, the "B Quadrant," is for people who build **business *systems*.** B quadrant people grow businesses that create residual income. A good example of this is a franchise. A franchise is a proven business model that can be purchased.

Network marketing would be another example of a B Quadrant business. The financial muscle of a B Quadrant business system comes from all the people at work. With both a franchise and network marketing, the owner benefits from both a proven business model and the productivity of a team.

"Leverage" is a term that describes accomplishing more with less. When you work with a team, you can serve more people in a compressed amount of time. It might take one person working alone forty hours to serve as many customers that a team can serve in one hour. A business system gives you the leverage of *OPT* (Other People's Time). OPT is what billionaire oil investor J. Paul Getty meant when he said, "I'd rather have one percent of the efforts of 100 people than 100 percent of my own efforts." Leveraging OPT describes how B Quadrant entrepreneurs think about making money.

The last quadrant is the "I Quadrant," which stands for Investor. This is the leverage of *OPM* (Other Peoples' Money). People in the I Quadrant put money to work. It might be their own money, or some else's money. They might own other businesses, precious metals, and paper assets like stocks and bonds. I Quadrant investors have the financial savvy to invest money to make more money. Warren Buffett is the quintessential I Quadrant investor.

Here's the point: We all operate more comfortably in one quadrant *versus* another. To begin, ask yourself in which quadrant you are most comfortable. And secondly, which quadrant do you *want* to be comfortable in? The point is awareness. Become aware of how you think about making money. If you're not sure what you believe, just watch what you do. What you *do* will show you what you really believe. Your life can change when you learn to think differently about making money.

After high school, I was an electrician in the E Quadrant. More recently, I have been in the S Quadrant as a physician in a private medical group. After the painful realization that I was working in the hospital too much, I wanted to move into the B Quadrant so I could gain more free time. You will soon understand how the B Quadrant can give you more free time as you keep reading.

If you don't like the results you have so far in your particular quadrant, you can change. If you are not satisfied with the amount of free time and money you have, you can choose to change quadrants. The power to change is your prerogative; it's your responsibility.

So to answer the question "Is a royalty-income business realistic for the average person?"—that depends on YOU. A royalty income IS realistic. It doesn't matter that you won't inherit an oil well or produce a blockbuster movie. What does matter is how you think about making money, and whether you are okay feeling uncomfortable while you learn new skills.

What I will show you in this book is a royalty income business that IS realistic for the average person. I see ordinary people creating extraordinary results because they follow a proven business system that works.

Many of us simply have not had the opportunity to marinate with the right concepts long enough. We can know something in our heads, but not allow it to penetrate our hearts. In order for new ideas about money to change our behavior, they must reside in the heart. Allowing these beliefs to take root and grow up takes time. It takes reading through books like this one, and pondering new ideas, especially the ones that challenge us.

The real gift of royalty income

So what does a royalty income really give you? An attorney might have a big bank account, but she might be missing out on her son's basketball games. An investment banker might be providing amply for his family's financial needs, but emotionally, they also need him present at their recitals and school plays. These people need more time. People miss that finite window of time left to care for a dying loved one. They miss their babies' first words, the first steps. People miss too many of the firsts, and the lasts.

This is called time poverty. This was me. Maybe it's also you.

What a residual income stream gives you is *more time*. When you step out of the left quadrants and into the right, you are changing your financial paradigms. Since you aren't continually selling your time in exchange for linear income, you can eventually end up with an income stream that isn't dependent upon your time to earn it. You will have learned how to create a beautiful thing called *recurring or royalty income.*

A royalty income can allow you to focus on other life priorities. Does working for money always need to be the dominant focus of our lives? Many of us love to work, to create, to provide value for others. But it sure is nice to have options and to change our focus if the need arises.

B Quadrant business ownership is the most realistic way for an average person to enjoy a life-changing royalty income. If you want more in life, and you're ready to move beyond the E or S Quadrants, but you're not sure how to do it, this book is for you. I will show you how to evaluate a business opportunity, and how to determine its likelihood for generating a life-changing royalty income. You must become savvy about some basic business principles to make this happen. Knowledge really is power when it's applied.

CHAPTER 2
How to Evaluate a Business

WHEN CHOOSING a royalty income business, there are three criteria to keep in mind to guide your decision. Network marketing trainer Tim Sales was very helpful for helping me understanding this.

1. Find a company in a growing industry.
2. Sell a unique and consumable product or service that you love.
3. Leverage—work with a team of people who all have the same incentives to grow.

Let me explain.

Growth Industry

What is an industry? Examples of industries are computer technology or IT, auto industry, restaurant industry, hotel or travel industry, or weight loss industry. An industry is a grouping of similar products or services.

Principle number one is to pick a company in a growing industry. At any given time in the economy, some industries are declining in sales, some are flat, and some are experiencing growth. Joining a company that is in a growing industry is like sailing with the wind at your back. Some sectors of the economy are growing faster than others because large numbers of people want that specific product or service. It will just make it easier for you to grow a profitable distribution network if your products or services are in increasingly high demand.

What if you had the biggest distribution network for VHS tapes in the year 2000? I don't care how good your sales department or customer service was, you'd be out of business today. That industry has collapsed. Stay clear of industries that are declining. Make the economic trend your friend.

What about fitness, vitamins, weight loss, and skin care products? The health and wellness industry is a growing industry today. Some experts predict that it could reach $1 trillion dollars in annual sales over the next ten years. The wellness industry is a healthy industry to be in. (Sorry for that.) Partnering with a company that offers nutritional supplements, weight loss and skin care products would be like sailing with a wind at your back.

Do you or your friends use nutritional products? Your social network can be an effective way to get an idea of which companies and product lines are gaining momentum in the marketplace.

You've likely heard the saying "a rising tide lifts all ships." When billions of dollars are flowing into a particular industry, it just makes it that much easier for you to succeed there. Don't work *against* big economic trends. Find a product line that is in strong demand. Then try those products and see if you can fall in love with them.

To summarize, principle number one is to find a company and product line that is in a growing industry group.

Unique and consumable products

Principle number two is to find a product or service that is both unique and consumable. If a product is unique, and you love it, you must return to the same place to buy more. If you sell a product or service that people like, you want them coming back to *you* to get more. You don't want them shopping at the local store to buy more of what they initially purchased from you. Since you educated them on the benefits of the product, you want to be paid for each time they use the product, year after year.

Why consumable? A consumable product or service is the wellspring of royalty income. A consumable product gets used up each month. Without a product or service that people consume, like getting to the bottom of a bottle, or a membership that expires every month, you must continually find new customers to sell to. Without consumable products or services, you are forced to sell, sell, sell forever to receive another paycheck.

I don't know about you, but if I'm going to do the work of selling something, I'd like to get paid at least a hundred times for that effort. Consumable means repeat sales. Consumable means you don't need to find new customers continually in order to get another paycheck. Are we clear on this point?

Think: How many times did your phone provider need to sell you to get you to pay every month? Probably just once. Then you automatically pay for the service over and over. This is what we are after, only without the employees, buildings and infrastructure of a phone company. Does a unique, consumable product like this sound hard to find? They are out there. If you don't already have a company, ask your friends what products they love. A high-demand, consumable product in a growing industry is what we are after.

Let's look at some examples. Many years ago, we purchased a set of Lifetime Cookware, pots and pans. They were expensive, and came with a lifetime guarantee. They would be *unique*, but not *consumable.* The nice lady who sold us the cookware has not visited our home ever since the initial sale. She made a one-time commission. To get another paycheck, she would have to make another sale to another family.

What about a hammer? A hammer is neither unique nor consumable. Unless your passion is hardware products, you don't want to sell a line of tools. They last for a really long time. I still have the hammer that was given to me as a sixteen-year-old electrician apprentice. And I wouldn't even know or care what brand my old one is, if I should ever happen to want a new one. A hammer is not unique, and it's definitely not consumable. Don't sell hammers.

What about coffee? Coffee could be unique, and it certainly is consumable. The problem with trying to sell coffee is that people can buy coffee just about anywhere. Unique? No. Consumable? Yes. Are you getting the idea?

What about wellness products? Wellness products like vitamins, skin care, and weight loss products are definitely consumable. They are consumed daily, and are repurchased every month if the consumer wants to continue benefiting. What about unique? That depends. Some wellness products have patents and are unique. The good news here is that if the consumer likes what the product does, and the product is unique, where are they headed to buy more? Bingo! Yes, you!

If you want to create a residual income, the best way is to find a unique, high-demand, consumable product. Make sure the product is in a growing industry so the demand for it will stay perpetually high.

Leverage: Working with a team

The last of the three criteria for picking a company is to find an opportunity to create leverage. Traditional companies have employees, which are a form of leverage for the company owner. For example, say you are the owner of a company, and you have 10 employees who each work 40 hours a week. This gives you, the owner, 400 hours of productivity in one week. 10 employees X 40 hours = 400 hours of productivity. This is a powerful form of leverage, and it explains how you could potentially create hundreds or thousands of hours of productivity even though you personally worked only 40 hours that week.

There is a downside to employees. If you have employees, you may eventually need a human resources department, because there will be drama. Who wants to deal with that? Plus, finding and keeping good employees is problematic.

Real estate brokers get a little closer to enjoying the marketplace leverage of employees without having to manage them. If you are the broker who has a dozen realtors selling property, you will benefit from the productivity of those 12 realtors. Real estate agents earn more as they sell more. Since the broker gains also, more sales and more earnings is a win-win situation for all parties involved. So far, so good.

The main flaw with the broker-agent relationship is this: What is a highly successful realtor able to do if she desires to have more leverage? She can leave the broker, and become her own broker. Nice. *Unless* you're the broker in the scenario, in which case, now you have just trained your competitor.

Here's a million dollar question (quite literally): *Is it possible to enjoy the productivity of employees without the hassle of actually having employees or the stress of managing payroll?* If it sounds like an absurd question, hang on. I would have said "nope" 10 years ago. I know better today. The answer is "yes!"

As you may have guessed, there is a business model available that offers the productivity of employees without actually having them. Network marketing is a business model where everyone on the team has the same or similar opportunities to grow their distribution network. This is an economically powerful, synergistic win-win for everyone. More on network marketing in the next chapter.

To find and service hundreds of customers, you must work with a team. There's no way around it. There are not enough hours in the day for one person alone to serve that many people. Your family will leave you if you try. Attempt it even for a season of life and it could ruin your marriage.

Let's review. The three primary criteria for identifying the best royalty income business are:

1. Find a growth industry. This is a sector of the economy that is attracting billions of dollars, and growing year after year.
2. Choose unique and consumable products that you love.
3. Have a system of leverage where everyone on the team has the same opportunity to grow their business.

When you truly grasp these factors, you will develop *conviction* about the company you've chosen. It's this conviction that people will hear in your voice when you tell them about what you're doing. It's the conviction in your voice that will attract the right people, the people who are looking for more in life—people like yourself.

While not all network marketing companies are created equally, the next chapter will explain how some can meet all three of of these criteria beautifully.

CHAPTER 3

What Is Network Marketing?

MOST PEOPLE WOULD AGREE that the best form of advertising is a happy customer. If you like a product or service, you might share it with your family, friends and coworkers. This is essentially how network marketing works. Your "network" refers to the people with whom you come into contact. "Marketing" is . . . well, it's marketing. It's advertising. It's making something known. It's explaining the benefits of something to someone who is interested.

So, when you combine the words "network" and "marketing," you are describing the activity of making a product or service known to potentially interested people around you. We do this often without thinking about it. We tend to share what we like with people we care about.

We share our favorite restaurants, movies, babysitters and vacation places. This is the best form of marketing on the planet—personal recommendations based on personal experience. Interestingly, it's also the least expensive form of marketing.

Some companies use network marketing as their primary method of educating customers about their products and services. Other names occasionally used to describe this form of marketing are:

Direct Sales
Direct Selling

Direct-to-Consumer Marketing
Person-to-Person Marketing
Word-of-Mouth Marketing
Multi-Level Marketing

The most common form of marketing is called "retail marketing." Think grocery stores, department stores and shopping malls here. With retail marketing, a company uses TV commercials, newspapers, magazines and billboards or internet ads to advertise their product or service. This illustration demonstrates the primary difference between retail marketing and network marketing.

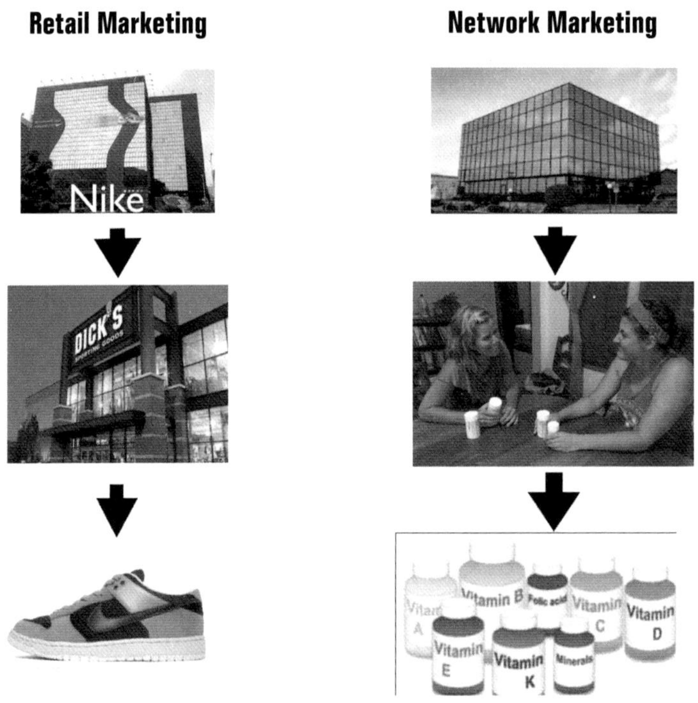

Do you see the main difference? The distinction is *who* or *what* does the advertising and selling. It could be a professional ad agency and a department store (retail sales), or it could be a satisfied customer (network marketing). That's the primary difference.

Retail sales is the dominant way products are sold. And it's also the most expensive way to move a product to a consumer. Approximately 85% of what you're paying to carry a product out of a store is covering the cost of marketing and distribution. With network marketing, the cost of getting the product into your hands is cut down closer to 50%.

So ask yourself: Which sales route can put a product into your hands at a better price? The fact is, I can buy a higher-quality nutritional product from my network marketing company than I can from a retail vitamin store. It's like buying wholesale *versus* retail. Why pay retail if you can shop wholesale?

In addition to lower cost, there is another important reason why a company would choose to distribute their products via network marketing over retail marketing. As economist Paul Pilzer explains, companies that offer "information-rich" products sometimes prefer network marketing. (An information-rich product requires some explanation for how it works.) Being educated by a trusted friend about how a product works is often more helpful than trying to figure everything out on your own. In our information-overloaded society, we often have too much content to sort through.

Years ago, when I was having some health challenges and looking for nutritional products, I was going to shop at the local heath food store. I would have paid more money for a lesser-quality product had I done that. Instead, a friend who'd had a first-hand experience with a brand of high-quality nutritional products (distributed *via* a network marketing company) was able to direct me. As a result, I received a more effective product at a better price.

Here's a common scenario with the personal approach of network marketing:

> Cathy: "I've tried all kinds of diets. I just can't seem to keep off the weight."
>
> Wendy: "Have you ever heard of the glycemic index?"
>
> Cathy: "No. What's that?"
>
> Wendy: "Well, the glycemic index tells you how quickly certain foods turn into sugar. If you switch to more low-glycemic foods, you can prevent your blood sugar from spiking, and keep the weight off. It all has to do with insulin—your fat storage hormone."

Cathy, "Hmmm. I never knew that. Does it really work?"

Wendy, "It does work. Have you noticed that I lost 30 pounds . . . and they haven't found me yet?"

Cathy: "Ha! I just figured you have more self-control than I do."

Wendy: "I've actually been able to help a lot of other people with this problem, too. Would you like me to email you some information about the low-glycemic meal-replacements I use? Or maybe we could sit down for coffee sometime to talk it through."

Cathy: "Absolutely! This is exactly what I need."

That kind of simple exchange happens every day. One person has a challenge. Another person knows of a potential solution and is willing to share it. That's called *helping.* That's also called *network marketing.* Good marketing is really about finding people with challenges and connecting them with solutions.

Since network marketers don't primarily get paid to physically *distribute* a product, some may wonder what they actually get paid for. While it's true that they may not distribute physical products, they actually distribute something more valuable than the actual product—information *about* the products.

Can you believe it?

Intellectual distribution

Economist Paul Zane Pilzer calls this more valuable form of distribution "intellectual distribution." He is describing how network marketers get paid to share accurate information about how a product works to people who can benefit from using that product. Accurate, relevant information delivery—*intellectual distribution*—is a major aspect of the value that network marketing adds to the marketplace. This is a big reason why people who like to teach can be so effective at network marketing.

This illustration depicts what marketing does. It opens up the bottleneck from the existing products/ideas to the marketplace that needs them. This is intellectual distribution at its finest.

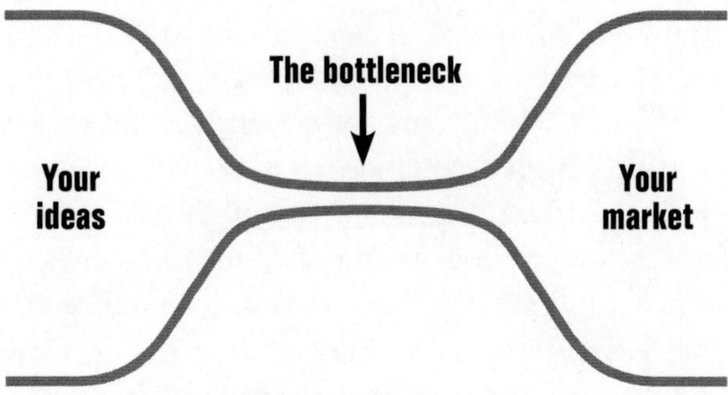

As you might guess from the illustration, whoever is most effective at opening up the bottleneck serves the most people. Whoever serves the greatest number of people earns the most money.

In a free-market economy, money is the natural by-product of serving others. Author and Rabbi Daniel Lapin calls money a "certificate of appreciation for having served another human being." Companies that utilize network marketing distribute over $130 billion of products and services annually around the world. That's a lot of certificates of appreciation flying around!

Think about it from the perspective of the company for a moment. Let's say you designed a product that you know works. You know many people could benefit from it. You have a choice regarding how you will bring your product to the marketplace. You can go the conventional route, retail marketing. Or you can go the unconventional route, network marketing.

With the retail route, you will need to hire a sales and marketing staff. You'll need to train employees how to care for the customers. These people who work for you may or may not actually use your product. Bottom line: You'll need to increase the cost of your product to cover the increased expenses associated with marketing and selling the product. This total cost could be as high as 85% of the cost of the product.

Your other option is to go the unconventional route, and let your happy customers do the legwork *for* you. People who love your product and have personal, compelling product stories become your workforce. You won't have to hire or fire any of your sales reps. Turnover will occur through natural attrition—some of your people may quit on their own, but you don't have to endure the employment drama.

By using network marketing as your sales and marketing model, you can keep the cost of the product lower because you have less expenses associated with moving the product to the end user. Lower cost combined with high quality equals more value for your customers. This is one reason why some experts believe that network marketing is the next evolutionary advancement in business marketing.

In the 1950s, a brand new business model came onto the scene. *Franchising.* At the time, the concept of franchising raised a lot of eyebrows. Many considered it an illegitimate way to do business. The United States government nearly made it illegal! Today, franchising is unarguably a brilliantly successful way to market products and services. New ideas can create new winners and new losers.

The Direct Selling Association (DSA) is an organization that offers ethical guidance and oversight for the network marketing industry. Here are some of the largest network marketing companies in 2014, according to directsellingnews.com:

Annual Sales

1	Amway	$11.80B
2	Avon	$9.95B
3	Herbalife	$4.80B
4	Vorwerk	$3.70B
5	Mary Kay	$3.60B
6	Natura	$3.20B
7	Nu Skin	$3.18B
8	Tupperware	$2.67B
9	Belcorp	$1.96B
10	Oriflame	$1.95B
11	Primerica	$1.27B
12	Ambit Energy	$1.20B
13	Telecom Plus	$1.10B
14	Stream Energy	$867M
15	Yanbal	$848M
16	Miki	$783M
17	Thirty-One	$763M
18	Blyth	$750M

19	USANA	$718M
20	ACN	$700M
21	New Era	$678M
22	Market America	$547M
23	Amore Pacific	$520M
24	Forbes Lux	$489M
25	Scentsy	$485M
26	AdvoCare	$460M
27	It Works! Global	$456M
28	Noevir Holdings	$455M
29	Isagenix	$448M
30	COSWAY	$440M
31	YoFoto	$428M
32	Arbonne	$413M
33	Better Way	$407M
34	Nature's Sunshine	$378M
35	For Days	$376M
36	Apollo	$340M
37	Team National	$332M
37	KK ASSURAN	$332M
39	Team Beachbody	$328M
40	LR Health & Beauty Sys	$323M
41	4Life	$300M
42	Longrich	$292M
43	PM-International	$284M
44	Neways	$280M
45	Viridian Energy	$267M
46	Jeunesse	$257M
47	North American Power	$256M
48	MENARD	$255M
49	Southwestern Advantage	$253M
50	Elken	$233M

According to Direct Selling Facts, there are over 17 million Americans who are involved in network marketing. Sales were over $34.5 billion in 2014, growing at 3% yearly. Those are healthy numbers and support the notion that plenty of people are succeeding in this newer, nontraditional form of entrepreneurship.

Network marketing is simply a more efficient way of getting the right information in front of the right person. For retail marketing, this is very expensive to accomplish. "Information transfer" is an overhead cost for every company. If a business can accomplish this marketing with less expense, it can pass along more value to the customer.

It's all about value

In a free-market economy, it's all about value. The company that offers the most quality for the best price is rewarded by the marketplace. And this is exactly what good network marketing companies do—offer quality products at a better price.

The company that gives more value to the consumer is the company that ultimately wins. That's why franchising couldn't be stopped; the value it added to the marketplace was undeniable. Today, network marketing is enduring a process of scrutiny and criticism similar to what franchising faced in the 1950s.

In the next chapter we will examine what to look for in a quality network marketing company.

CHAPTER 4
The Ideal Network Marketing Company

IN CHAPTER 2, we discussed how to evaluate a business opportunity in general. We looked at three important criteria:

1. **Is the company in a growing industry?** Is there a steadily increasing demand for your products or services? Are there billions of dollars chasing after the products or services you represent? You don't want to dive into a flat or declining market. Remember the VCR/VHS industry? Ancient history now. Research current market trends, and "make the trend your friend."

2. **Is the product or service both unique *and* consumable?** You want unique so that happy customers keep coming back exclusively to *you* to get more product. Once you spend time educating people, you don't want to lose that investment when your customer goes off and buys the same product somewhere else. You want consumable products, so your customers use up their inventory every month, and buy more. Otherwise, you will need to keep on selling in order to keep a paycheck coming in. Repeat sales is the fountainhead of a royalty income business.

3. **Does the company offer a system of leverage?** Traditional business accomplishes leverage *via* paid employees. You only

have so many hours in a day. Therefore, you don't want to get paid just for your efforts alone. You want to be paid based upon the productivity of a team *who all have the same opportunities to succeed.* An advantage with network marketing companies is that you usually work with a team. If you teach 10 people how to teach 10 people to do what you do, that amounts to a team of 100 people. 10 X 10 = 100, right? What if those 100 people each teach 10 more people? Now you have 1,000 people. Even if half quit, you still end up with a sizable team. The leverage effect is basic math. It's as straightforward as 5 X 5 X 5 X 5 = 625.

These are the big three. You have the wind at your back if your company meets the above three requirements. Now let's get more specific to selecting a company within the network marketing industry as a whole.

4. **Pick a company with products or services that you love.** I can't overstate the importance of this. If you don't absolutely love and believe in your products, you won't convey in your voice the sincerity that attracts people. I'm not talking about being a cheerleader; you need to be sincerely passionate for your personality type. If you love a product or service, it's natural to want to share it with others. If you can't easily think of people who would benefit from using your product or service, you may not have found the right company yet.
5. **Pick a company whose leadership you respect.** A company is only as good as the team who leads it. Make every effort to learn who the executive team is. What is their background? What experiences do they bring to the team? Do they seem like men and women of integrity?
6. **Fiscal accountability.** If your prospective company is publicly-traded, you are granted an additional level of comfort that the financials you see are trustworthy. Public companies must declare their financials to the Security and Exchange Commission. Accountability is a good thing.
7. **Choose a company with a track record of success.** In the

direct sales industry, new companies are launched all the time. What is the five-year survival rate of a brand new company? Not good. Every company had to be new at some time, so I'm not saying to avoid all new companies. But you'll be investing lots of time and energy, so you don't want your company going broke. Look for a company that has a solid multi-year track record of success.

8. **It helps to pick a company with a great story.** The more interesting the story, the better. Everyone loves a good story. You're going to tell your company's story over and over, so make it a good one. In the marketplace, it always helps to distinguish yourself from the herd.

9. **Choose a company with a fair compensation plan.** You want a company that will pay you well for your time and energy. Some companies will report this number as a percentage of total sales. For top shelf companies, this number can approach 50%. Do some research. Bottom line: The company needs to make a profit; the corporate team needs to be paid well in order to attract and keep talent; if the company is publicly-traded, the shareholders need to be paid. The financials must work well for everyone, for the long-term. Some network marketing companies have been profitable for decades. Look for a company characterized by a long history of doing the right thing for all parties involved.

10. **Some network marketing companies offer a *perpetuity clause*.** This is a legal term that means that, in the event of your death, your business would go to your children or other benefactors. If you spend years building a royalty income business, you want to pass that legacy along to whomever you choose. A perpetuity clause gives you this power.

11. **Finally, you want a network marketing company that handles the logistics:**

    - Distributes the products so you don't need to carry an inventory or spend time delivering products. Driving around town with products in your trunk is NOT a great business model.

- Collects payments, administrates finances, and cuts you a weekly commission check.
- Creates high-quality marketing tools to help you explain the company and products.
- Hosts outstanding live events for all the associates on a regular basis.
- Handles all the legal issues to protect your business.

These eleven criteria are met by *many network marketing* companies. Don't settle. Find a company that you feel confident with, whose products you love and use daily. Then get to work for at least five years. Don't jump ship whenever a friend shows you a new opportunity. If your company meets the above criteria, stick with it. If you don't love your products, or your company is missing some of the above criteria, you may want to keep looking.

The Direct Sales Association website is a good place to look if you want to research the industry. See www.dsa.org.

Some people will carefully analyze dozens of companies before selecting one they like. Andrea and I partnered with the first company we looked at. Everyone's different. Do your homework. Sample the products. Meet other reps. Visit the home office. Attend events. If you like what you see, then get started. Most companies will require new reps to purchase a business starter kit, and a sampling of the products. This may cost anywhere from $50 to $2,000, depending upon the company. The initial cost of getting started is generally considered a business expense, so it may be tax-deductible.

In the next chapter, we will look at what some business experts have to say about network marketing.

CHAPTER 5

What Experts Say About Network Marketing

ROBERT KIYOSAKI and Donald Trump have this to say in their book *Why We Recommend Network Marketing*:

> We found one business model that stood out from the rest. This particular business creates passive income and can be operated on a flexible, part-time basis. This business model is called *Network Marketing.*

Thank goodness a distribution network can be built part-time. When I first started to grow my business, I was a full-time anesthesiologist working 60 to 80 hours a week, married, and the father of four children. I didn't have "free time." I simply chose to redirect some of my wasted minutes normally spent sitting in the doctor's lounge waiting for the next surgery to start. Instead, I would find a quiet place in the hospital to make a few phone calls. A favorite time of mine was the hour or two after our kids went to bed. Most weeks, I could carve out somewhere between five to ten hours to work on *my* business.

> You're either building your own network, or spending your life building someone else's network.
>
> —Robert Kiyosaki, *The Business of the 21st Century*

We are all the part of *some* distribution network helping to move a product or service to customers. The distribution of goods and services is the lifeblood of business. Products or services flow out, and income flows in. Just about every business functions *via* some network. It might be helpful to ask yourself what aspect of a network you are already a part of. Like Kiyosaki says, you're already helping to build someone else's network; maybe it's time to start building your own?

Network marketing is the ideal business model for an average person who has above-average dreams. As you engage the process, you will learn new skills. It's the skills you learn that eventually create value for the marketplace. This is how you can build a legitimate business that will continue to pay you for years to come.

What would your life look like if you were to add an additional $1,000 or $2,000 a month of residual income? What would you do with the money? Would you travel? Would you buy a home or new car? Would you send your parents on a vacation? Would you go back to school? Would you pay off some debt? Would you give more? Maybe you want more free time. Whatever your dream, the process can begin for you today.

In his book *The Next Millionaires*, Paul Zane Pilzer writes about network marketing as one of three major trends converging to create "a perfect storm of unprecedented economic opportunity."

Pilzer identifies three global trends:

1. **Major growth in the wellness industry.** More and more people are choosing to be proactive with their health instead of reactive. Wellness products would include things like nutritional supplements, meal replacement foods, skin care products, and fitness centers.

2. **Affordable technology.** Today's smart phones can compete technologically with the most powerful computers that only the biggest companies of the past had—and individual access to smart phones and other tech is increasing exponentially every day.

3. **Network Marketing.** The direct-to-consumer marketing industry is growing rapidly. More companies than ever are

opting to bring their products to market by using the more efficient model of network marketing.

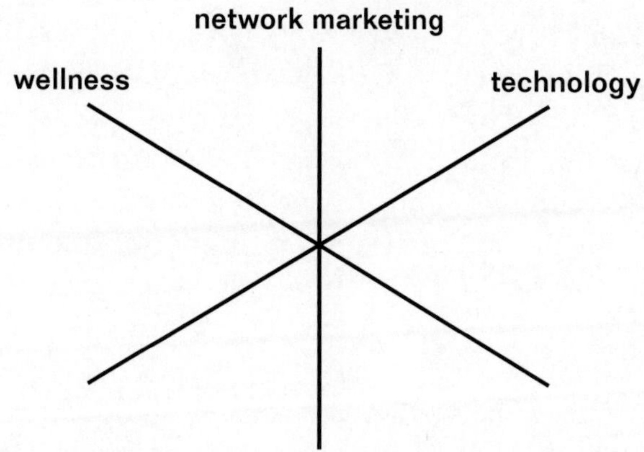

The convergence of these three trends creates an economic "perfect storm" according to Pilzer. This phenomenon helps to explain the dramatic business success that regular, everyday people—with no prior business experience—are enjoying with network marketing. Average people are creating significant royalty incomes with no prior business experience. And this is happening with part-time effort during challenging economic times.

> Home-based businesses are one of the fastest-growing segments in our economy, and that trend will only continue as the age of the corporation, which began barely a century ago, now gives way to the age of the entrepreneur.
>
> —Paul Pilzer, *The Next Millionaires*

There are heart surgeons, rocket scientists, attorneys, conventional business owners, stay-at-home moms, military officers, teachers, real estate developers, carpenters—you name the occupation—involved in network marketing today. What Dr. Stephen Covey has observed is certainly true—network marketing is quickly becoming a viable path of entrepreneurship for many.

> I think network marketing has come of age. It's become undeniable that it's a viable way to entrepreneurship and independence for millions of people.
>
> —Dr. Stephen Covey, *The 7 Habits of Highly Effective People*

Open-minded people of all walks of life are benefitting from this newest advancement in business franchising. Network marketing has been referred to as a "personal franchise." What that means is instead of needing to acquire the expenses of buildings and employees associated with traditional franchising, the franchise in this case is *you*. You are the walking, talking, living, breathing "personal" franchise. It may be hard to believe, but one person with a smart phone today can compete with the biggest businesses of yesterday.

> The future of network marketing is unlimited. There's no end in sight. It will continue to grow, because better people are getting into it.
>
> —Brian Tracy, author and motivational speaker

Some of our closest friends today are our business colleagues. We share the same values of faith, family, health, personal growth, and entrepreneurship. How many occupations exist where you can choose your own coworkers and work environment? What kind of a work atmosphere and team culture would you prefer? Can you imagine working with your best friends?

The late legendary business coach Jim Rohn said, "Network marketing is the big wave of the future. It's taking the place of franchising, which now requires too much capital for the average person . . . . [With it,] I was able to work full-time on my job, and part-time on my fortune."

A part-time network marketing business might grow so large that having a primary "day job" becomes optional. What a wonderful option to have! Many people love their day job and would never dream of leaving it. For others, the day job is sucking the life right out of them. Having a secondary income stream simply gives us more options.

Another benefit of network marketing is that you can learn from people who are already successful. In how many industries can you find successful entrepreneurs gladly revealing their business secrets to neophytes just getting started? How many new business opportunities come with a successful mentor to guide you? Network marketing does.

You may be asking yourself, if network marketing is so good, why don't more people do it? Great question. Well, there are some disadvantages. Here's one drawback that network marketing trainer Eric Worre describes as "the 'Catch' to network marketing: You must accept a temporary loss of social esteem from ignorant people."

Would losing the admiration of a few people be a problem for you? The truly unfortunate thing is that some folks cannot handle even a temporary loss of "social esteem." Some people are so dependent on the affirmation of their peer group that their fragile egos cannot tolerate being misunderstood or ridiculed. This is a real barrier for some people. Not everyone has the internal fortitude to be an economic pioneer.

Business trainer Dani Johnson says it like this: "You can have a big bank account or a big ego; not both." So true! What would you rather have? I'll take the bank account, please.

> In most Americans' minds, it's a scam—questionable or unethical at best, immoral and illegal at worst. Many own-your-own entrepreneurial hopefuls have been hyped into turning over their life savings, only to see the company go out of business, taking their dreams down with them. There is even a move in Congress to outlaw it altogether!

Ironically, the above remarks are not referring to network marketing. They are from the 1960s, addressing the business model of *franchising*! Can you believe it? Franchise operations were so strongly denigrated! McDonalds, Pizza Hut, Subway, Chipotle.

But now . . . the naysayers' scoffing and scorn have been put to rest—for good. There are one million franchise businesses in existence today, contributing nearly $1 trillion to the U.S. economy. Yet there was a time when this emerging business model was nearly outlawed!

> [Direct selling] is an industry that helps you develop confidence, and it really prepares people for the new economy.

> There is now no such thing as job security. What direct sales really does is it teaches you how to begin to secure your own future, so that you're not going through life living fearfully, worried about whether you will be replaced by technology or whether your job is outsourced.
>
> —Les Brown, author and motivational speaker

Les Brown teaches audiences around the world that the best way to create a better economic future is to work hard on *yourself.* Direct sales will teach you things you never realized about yourself—your self-imposed limitations, your undeveloped strengths. You get adept at seeing potential in others, at motivating and leading them toward their goals. You can develop your speaking and listening skills. Growing a direct sales business is inherently its own personal development curriculum.

Most people who have built large networking businesses will tell you that the personal growth they experienced was the most valuable part of the journey. Sure, the money is great, and can buy you more free time and wonderful experiences, but growing as a person is priceless. Increasing your capacity to serve more people because of the person you have become is a satisfaction that no money can buy. It is deeply rewarding to be able to face things confidently today that used to scare you yesterday. This kind of personal metamorphosis can happen to you.

The marketplace pays for one thing: Value. Value is making someone's life better. How can you increase your ability to add more value to the marketplace? By learning new skills. There are no shortcuts. Network marketing gives you a path to follow *at your own pace.* It provides mentors to guide you. It gives you a supportive environment to encourage you and to hold you accountable. You can go slowly, or you can go quickly. It's completely up to you. Everyone's situation is unique. Some people have ten hours a week to invest, while others have forty hours a week. The speed at which you progress is entirely up to you.

Growing a network marketing business is a completely customized personal development curriculum for helping you develop skills that create value for others. Skills increase your capacity to serve others more effectively. Forget about whether you attended college or not. Forget about whether you have business or sales experience or not. Forget about whether you can get a large line of credit from the bank. Forget about all that. It doesn't matter here.

Direct sales rewards one thing very well—your attitude. Will you be teachable and engage the process? Will you do what your mentor recommends? Will you learn from those who have already done what you want to do? Will you hang in there when it gets hard? That's really what matters. That's the admission price—your attitude.

Network marketing is not perfect. No industry is. And it's certainly not a good fit for everyone. But this I do know—if you want to own your own business, network marketing has plenty of good to offer, with far less risk than anything else out there.

No shortcuts. No something-for-nothing. No get-rich-quick. It's all hard work, discipline, vision, perseverance, and following instruction. Most good things are upstream. This is how you know something is real and not a scam. Good things aren't usually easy, and easy things aren't usually good. This is how life works.

From whom will you take advice? From your friend who has never built a business? From your coworkers who live paycheck to paycheck? Whose opinion will you value most when it comes to launching your own business? You just read what some of the most successful entrepreneurs and thought leaders have concluded about network marketing.

If you're wise, you won't give much weight to the opinions of those who have never accomplished what you're trying to do. If you planned to climb a mountain, would you ask someone for advice who has never climbed anything? That would be silly, wouldn't it? And yet this is exactly what I see people do when they are thinking this through.

There are powerful *financial* advantages when it comes to having your own business— advantages that, unfortunately, very few people understand. The next chapter will explain what they are and how you can harness their power.

CHAPTER 6
The Financial Accelerators

OWNING A NETWORK marketing business offers three major financial advantages. I call them "financial accelerators" because they accelerate the amount of money that flows from your business into your bank account. It's easier to paddle a canoe downstream than upstream. Flying with the wind is faster than flying against it. These examples describe *natural* advantages. Growing a royalty income business offers similar *financial* advantages.

The three unique financial benefits of a royalty income business are leverage, a residual-income business model, and tax breaks that favor business ownership.

Leverage

Webster's Dictionary defines leverage as "the increase in force gained by using a lever." Okay. Not super-exciting, but when it comes to business, a powerful lever is *OPT* (Other People's Time). Of course, we want the benefits of having employees without the hassle of actually managing them.

Network marketing is a business model that enjoys the leverage of *OPT*, without the downside of having workers to manage. When you find a business system where everyone has the same opportunities to grow their income, you have found something that has immense economic power. You have found a lever that can create tremendous wealth, almost unrealistic wealth.

For example, it took me 13 years of training beyond high school, and $300,000 in education expenses (today's dollars) to earn the professional income *I matched with my royalty income business in just six years!* And I have been receiving that professional-level income for the past year while working as a missionary in Honduras! Suspend your disbelief for a moment and keep reading.

How does a corporate CEO earn 100X as much as the average employee? The answer has to be that the CEO benefits from a portion of the productivity of all the workers below him in the chain of command. Even if the CEO puts in *twice* as many hours as the average employee how does he become *100X* times more "productive?" The lever in this example is OPT. He is paid on the productivity of every employee in the organization. While most people won't become CEO of a big company, network marketing gives us a similar economic advantage.

This numeric breakdown is helpful for understanding the economic power of many people at work, which we will call a "team." It explains mathematically what actually happens when we leverage OPT. Look at the left-hand column. It breaks down how many hours you will "sell" to the marketplace in a scenario where you get paid for *your work only.* In one week, you may work 50 hours. If you do this for 50 weeks a year, you work 2,500 hours in one year. Over a 40-year career, you will be paid one time for your 100,000 hours of productivity, which you sold to the marketplace.

Understanding Leverage

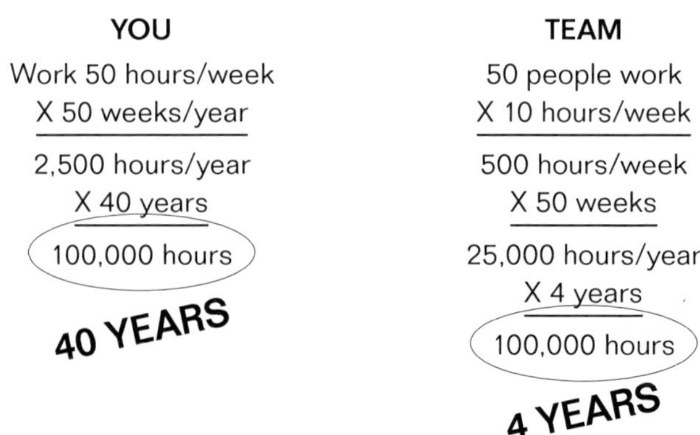

50 X 50 = 2,500 X 40 = 100,000 hours.

In the right-hand scenario, you work with a TEAM of 50 people. If 50 people in your team each work 10 hours a week, that equals 500 hours of productivity in one week. If this is done for 50 weeks a year, that is 25,000 hours of productivity in one year. After four years, this amounts to 100,000 hours of marketplace productivity.

Do you see how powerful this is? By working with a team of network marketers, you can produce the same amount of service for the marketplace in *four years* that a person working alone will produce in 40 years! Seemingly unbelievable, but true. It's the advantage of many people at work. It helps to explain how a CEO can appear to be 100X more "productive."

A team of ten, twenty or fifty people can serve many more customers than one person can who works really hard. Hence, the first financial accelerator, leverage, allows the owner of a network marketing business to serve a greater number of people in a shorter amount of time. This results in massively increased productivity, which translates into more earnings from your business.

Residual Income

The second financial accelerator is residual income. As we've learned, residual income occurs when you sell a consumable product. Believe it or not, some network marketing companies offer products that people want to repurchase monthly, over and over and over. It's almost as good as owning the rights to an oil well.

Hitting the time barrier

Here's the deal—we all need a roof over our heads. We need to eat; we need to take care of our families; we need to do some recreational things; we want to keep learning; and we want to be generous and give. This is part of what it means to be human. Because of this reality, we need money. Most of us were taught that the plan to earn money was to get good grades in school, go to college, and get a high-paying job. And there is absolutely nothing wrong with that. But most of us grew up thinking that was the *only* way. To divert from that traditional path would raise eyebrows, right?

Here's a major problem with the traditional plan: To earn a linear income means we will always be selling our most precious resource—time. When we are young, maybe single and without children, we don't mind working long hours for money. What happens to many of us eventually is that we have more demands on our time, we grow weary running on the hamster wheel for money. We begin to realize that our time on Earth is short. We realize that we aren't spending enough time with the people we love, or not spending enough time doing the things that we love.

We have all heard of planes hitting the sound barrier. My good friend Daniel calls this realization of running out of time as "hitting the *time* barrier." We recognize that we simply don't have enough time to serve the customers we need to serve in order to earn the money we need earn. Too many needs, not enough time.

I hit the time barrier at age 40. It occurred one night while I was working at the hospital. We routinely worked 24-hour shifts. It was late at night and I was exhausted. I missed my family. I felt like my kids were growing up without me. There wasn't enough time. Have you heard the expression, "When the student is ready, the teacher arrives?" Well, this student was ready. I was receptive for the provocative ideas that would soon rock my world. Maybe you are ready.

Some of us begin to question the traditional plan of "go to college and get a job," and work hard for the next forty years earning only linear income. How many intelligent, hardworking people ever learn about residual income? A royalty-income business is the only realistic, part-time way I am aware of to break the time barrier. Residual income allows you to break the time barrier because it allows you to abandon the longstanding requirement that you must always lose time to gain money.

Get this: *With network marketing you can still have money flowing in every week, even if you choose to stop working.* Can you imagine a life like that? How would your life change? What would you do differently if you had all the time and money you needed? What has always seemed impossible just became possible. Because of residual income, you now have enough time *and* money. Congratulations, you just broke the time barrier!

Properly valuing our most precious commodity—time—is the primary motivation I see in those who grow a successful royalty income business. When we recognize how there simply isn't enough time to accomplish what we want to in life, we become open to other ideas. Some of us even become open to non-traditional options like the one I'm describing here.

Your decision to embrace different ideas may run counter to what your friends think. Be prepared for this. Like crabs pulling each other back into a slowly boiling pot of water, your well-intentioned peer group may discourage you. Independent thinkers are always challenged by the mainstream.

Daren Hardy describes it like this, "When you leave the herd, the herd will turn on you."

Here's a plan to break the time barrier:

1. Invest time and energy to learn network marketing.
2. Develop the discipline of delayed gratification; remember, you will be "working for free" when you start out.
3. Grow your royalty income business to the level of income you need.
4. Enjoy the extra time you now have, because money is flowing in regardless of whether you "go to work" or not.

This is ***not*** a fairy tale. It is happening all over the world. *You* could be next.

I never took my first three kids to school, or picked them up afterwards. I was too busy working. For our fourth child, guess who took him to school and picked him up? That's right. *I* did! I finally had that option. Since I began my business, I have enjoyed many wonderful experiences with my children—all because I was able to break the time barrier. That's the power of royalty income.

Residual income is the second "financial accelerator." Selling consumable products is the fountainhead of a royalty income business. Because of repeat sales, more money can flow from your business to your bank account *per customer* if you market a consumable product line.

Tax-favored income

The third and final financial accelerator is a favorable tax status for business owners. When it comes to tax deductions, it is beneficial to be an entrepreneur. Most people don't know that there are essentially two tax codes in the America. One is for employees, and the other is for business owners.

Most people are W2 employees. This means that the state and federal government both get a slice of your income before you do. If you are an employee, your earned income is the highest-taxed income. This means you pay a greater percentage of your income in taxes than people who own businesses do. Are you okay with this?

Business owners, independent contractors, and consultants are paid directly by the company to whom they provide services. At the end of the tax year, the company issues both the consultant and the IRS a tax form called a 10-99. It reports how much money the company paid out to the consultant over the year.

Let's compare how much an employee pays in taxes compared to a business owner: For illustrative purposes, let's see how earning $1,000 is taxed differently when both the employee and business owner purchase a personal computer (PC).

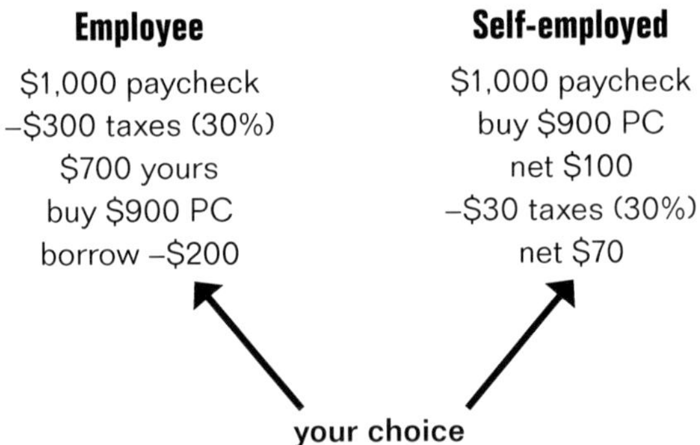

Do you see how an employee who earns $1,000 ends up borrowing $200, and paying $300 in taxes? Compare this to the business owner who also earns $1,000. The business owner buys the same personal computer for $900, and only pays $30 in taxes. This assumes a 100% business deduction for the expense of the personal computer.

Both employees and business owners purchase many of the same things like computers, cell phones, cell phone plans, internet services, books, meals, travel, *etc.*. The difference for the business owner is that most of these expenses can be "written off" pre-tax as business expenses. In comparison, the employee must buy these same items *with money that has already been taxed.*

Let me ask you a question: Would you rather buy things *before* your money is taxed, or *after* it gets taxed? Exactly. You get to keep more of your money if you can legally spend it *before* the government takes its cut.

This is why the third financial accelerator is tax protection *via* business ownership. This is another example of how more money will flow from your business to your bank account because of the tax advantages associated with business ownership.

Of course, I need to add the disclaimer here that you should follow up with your tax professional to gain a deeper understanding of eligibility details and proper handling. I am not a tax consultant, so I am not sharing this as though it were professional advice.

To recap, the financial accelerators are leverage, a residual-income business model, and tax breaks that favor business ownership. Like flying with the wind, they give you significant economic advantages, and yet most people are unaware they even exist.

In order to build a royalty income business you will need to learn new skills. The next chapter will explain the unique skill set required to serve people effectively with your network marketing business.

CHAPTER 7

Skills for Success, Part I

IF YOU WERE to ask me what the requirements are to becoming an anesthesiologist, I could sum it up for you pretty easily: Four years of college, four years of medical school, and four or five years of residency. Twelve or thirteen years of training combined with $300,000 in educational expenses—and then you could practice anesthesia.

Here's something that may be hard to believe: With part-time effort, it's entirely possible to earn more *royalty income* with network marketing than physicians who work very long hours with high liability.

Will it take you twelve years and cost $300,000 to learn the skills of network marketing? No. But it will cost you something.

Whether you are a physician or you are building a virtual distribution network, no one creates significant value for others without first acquiring skills. *And it will always cost time, money, and energy to get those skills.* If anyone tells you something different, beware. Network marketing is not a get-rich-quick pipe dream. Unfortunately, many people treat it that way, and they are always the ones who fail. And usually they leave behind a trail of unhappy business partners who feel taken advantage of.

So what skills do you need? When it comes to network marketing, the top six skills would be:

1. **Be interested in others**
2. **Find out what people want**
3. **Invite**
4. **Present the company story**
5. **Close and follow up**
6. **Clarify your VISION**

The first skill centers on being more interested in others than needing to impress them. Remember how Zig Ziglar said that if you first help enough people get what they want, you can have whatever you want? This is what skill #1 is all about. It's being more interested in the person you're talking to than your need to impress them. This is much easier said than done.

This first skill essentially describes a rare character trait called *humility*. I don't mean humility in the sense that you think little of yourself, or that you put yourself down in front of others. I'm thinking along the lines of how C.S. Lewis describes a humble person in his book *Mere Christianity*.

> Do not imagine that if you meet a really humble man he will be what most people call "humble" nowadays: he will not be a sort of greasy, smarmy person, who is always telling you that, of course, he is nobody.
>
> Probably all you will think about him is that he seemed a cheerful, intelligent chap who took a real interest in what you said to him.
>
> If you do dislike him, it will be because you feel a little envious of anyone who seems to enjoy life so easily. He will not be thinking about humility: he will not be thinking about himself at all.

Humility enables people to take more interest in the people around them. They can do this because they simply aren't thinking about themselves very much. It's helpful to think of humility as self-forgetfulness. The more you forget about yourself, the more aware you can become of what is happening around you.

Now, it's natural that we want to make a good first impression. First impressions are lasting impressions. In his classic book *How to Win Friends and Influence People,* Dale Carnegie teaches that every person has an inherent need to feel special and important.

Here's the point: If you are aware of the need *you have* to feel special and important, you can voluntarily put that desire aside.

This intentional "others-focus" is graduate-level self-awareness. Most people never learn this. If you develop this level of self-awareness, you are able to suppress your natural impulse to share your cool story first, which frees you up to listen to someone else's story instead. You are able to put your agenda aside for the moment. You can be mentally present to find others' needs, instead of being distracted with your own needs.

So skill #1 is being interested in others.

Skill #1: Be interested in others
Skill #2: Find out what people want

Here's how I teach skill #2: ***FORM*** is a useful mnemonic that stands for ***F****amily,* ***O****ccupation,* ***R****ecreation,* ***M****essage.*

When you are talking with your family and friends, your "warm market," you already know what they want. The first three of letters of FORM come in handy when getting to know someone new, your "cold market."

Family

When getting to know new people, a nice place to start is to ask them about their family. Married or dating? Kids? You will learn a lot by talking about family. They will likely ask you about your family, too. This is not an interview. You are simply getting better acquainted—you are listening for what matters most to people, and for what might be missing from their lives. Does Alicia feel like she has enough time for her husband, her kids, for herself? Is Dan worried about how he's going to provide for future expenses, like helping the kids with college or saving for retirement?

Occupation

Next, the conversation could move to work life: Ask people what they do for a living. How *long* have they done it? Do they *like* it? Do they like the contribution their work allows them to make? Do they ever think about doing something else? You are listening for what might be missing, or for what they want to change about their occupation.

Recreation

Depending on how the conversation has been going, you could transition into talking about hobbies. What do they do in their free time? Do they travel? Do they even *have* free time? Depending upon the rapport you build, you may or may not go very deep. It depends. It depends on their personality. It depends on whether the person is pressed for time.

The fastest way to build rapport is find something you share in common. There is a deeper relational connection that occurs when your life journey overlaps someone else's journey. It's hard to explain, but easy to recognize when it happens.

Now understand, these topical questions are not a scripted interview, and they do not have to follow a strict format. There should be give and take, back and forth. It's a sincere conversation where you really are interested. You are just getting to know them, and you want to determine whether you can serve them with your business or not.

Once you've explored these three F-O-R categories, LISTENED to the answers, and contributed to the dialogue, there is a good chance you will discern what matters most. You might know what they like—and don't like—about their lives. You might learn what's missing in their lives.

Often, you will discover needs that you can help them solve. With practice, you will be able to discern whether people are merely complaining, or if they truly want a solution. Are they *solution-oriented*? That is, are they ready to *do something* about the challenges they face? Do they really want to improve their lives, or are they just venting? If you sense they are really looking for a solution, you could offer an invitation, the "message"—the M in F-O-R-**M**.

Which brings us to Skill #3, making an invitation to take a look at a solution.

Skill #1: Be interested in others
Skill #2: Find out what people want
Skill #3: Invite

Let's say we are getting to know each other at a social function. You would learn that I enjoy being an anesthesiologist, but spend too much time at the hospital. I miss my kids and fear that I will have regrets if I don't make some changes to my schedule.

If you were FORMing me you could then say something like, "Have you ever considered building a residual income stream, which could free up more time down the road?" Of course, I wouldn't know what you were talking about, but your question might pique my interest. If you are a good listener, you would have discovered that I enjoy reading. You could then ask me if I was open to reading a book about residual income, maybe one of Robert Kiyosaki's books, or a book like the one you are reading now. If I felt you were credible, I would probably be curious enough to read it. You would then schedule a follow-up time for us to meet for coffee, and discuss the book.

Two weeks later we meet for coffee.

> You: "So Steve, what did you find most interesting about the book?"
>
> Steve: "I liked learning about how most people have only liabilities, which are costly, and how some people build assets, which produce something impressive called residual income."
>
> You: "Why does that interest you?"
>
> Steve: "I suffer from a serious condition called time poverty, blah, blah, blah . . . ."
>
> You: "Do you see why I thought you might be interested in learning about how to create income without always trading your time to earn it?"

Your last question shows that you were really listening to me, and you are suggesting a solution to my problem of not having enough time. Maybe your solution will work for me, or maybe not. You are only the messenger.

This is "intellectual distribution" at its finest. You are helping to transfer new concepts into my brain, and seriously messing with my paradigm about how money is created. This could then lead to a conversation about a real-life business model that creates residual income—network marketing!

Here's another scenario. The invite could go like this: "Hey Bill, you know how you've talked about buying real estate to create an extra income stream? Well, I found something that pays well with a lot less risk than real estate. Let's sit down sometime and I'll show you what it is."

There are many different ways to invite someone to take a look at your business or products. It's a good idea to memorize a couple invite lines that seem natural for you. Learn them so well that they roll off your tongue. You don't want to fumble around on the invitation. One of my favorite invite lines is, "Are you open to looking at something outside of what you're currently doing?" Many people who are in my business today took an initial look because of that simple question. What "solution-oriented" person wouldn't be open to "taking a look" at something?

Let's review: FORM stands for Family, Occupation, Recreation, Message. This mnemonic guides you to find what is missing in someone's life.

Once you learn these first two skills of taking a sincere interest in others, and being able to find out what they want, you will forever be expanding your relational world. And some of the people you meet will want to make changes in their lives *just like you did.*

Hold on. I can hear some of you protesting: "I'm introverted! I'm shy! I can't just walk up to a stranger and start talking."

Look, I am basically shy and introverted too. Your temperament or personality has nothing to do with this. We are talking about skills that can be learned. If I asked you to sit down and play the piano, and you never played before, you'd give me an odd look.

Learning any skill takes *practice.* FORMing people is a skill like learning to ski, or playing an instrument, or cooking. A skill is a skill. You practice it; you can learn it; you can teach it.

Here's an exercise I give new business partners who are having a hard time with the FORMing process. I will ask them to get acquainted with people using just the FOR (family, occupation, recreation) part of FORM. Leave off the Message or invitation, since that's the hardest part of the process (because it can provoke rejection). So you just spend time getting to know people without the pressure of inviting them to look at anything.

Here's what it looks like: Let's say you are at Starbucks. You might ask the server, "How long have you worked here?"

> She says, "Five years."
>
> You say, "Wow, that's a long time. You must *really* love it here."
>
> Her: "Not really. I'd rather get into something else."
>
> You: "Like what?"
>
> Her: "Like have my own company . . . be my own boss."
>
> You: "That sounds great. I've started my own business, and it's working out really well."
>
> Her: "Wow. That's really cool. I wish I could do something like that. I'm just not sure where to start."

Did you notice that you left off the **Invite** part of the process? You simply found out if the server enjoyed her job. That's all. No pressure to ask her to "look at something outside of working at Starbucks".

One more example: Let's say you've just finished up your work at a coffee shop. You stand up and close your laptop as you prepare to leave. You make brief eye contact with a man who has been sitting next to you for the past hour. You might say, "Great place to get some work done."

If he's open to conversation, he will contribute. If he's in a hurry, or closed to conversation, you'll be able to tell by his response. You may chat for a few minutes, or not. It all depends.

Growing your relational network is all about being in the habit of *noticing* what's happening around you, and being *intentional* to meet new people as you live your life. You simply stop to take an interest in others. Engage them in conversation, and see where it goes. Sometimes it goes nowhere; sometimes you make a new friend; sometimes the new friend becomes a new business partner. If you think that would never happen, think again. It happens all the time.

In life, we get what we look for. I look for business partners. Guess whom I tend to find?

When you "invite" people, you are simply giving them the opportunity to review information as it relates to their needs. When you invite them, you are demonstrating that you heard their needs, and you're offering a solution. Sharing this message is a way to honor them. You are offering to help. Your business may be for them; or it may not. Nothing more. Nothing less.

Here is something that can be very difficult about this process: *You must remain emotionally detached from their answer.* If you want to ride a miserable rollercoaster, become emotionally addicted to hearing people say "yes." Some *will* say "yes." Some will say "no." You can't control their responses. Your job is to find the need and to make the invite. "Would you like to review some information that could help you with that?" Yes or no. Detached. Then move on.

Daniel Goldman, psychologist and *New York Times* best selling author of *Emotional Intelligence*, states that the most influential people have a keen awareness of their own and other's emotions. Emotional intelligence (EI) is defined as the ability to recognize one's own and other people's emotions. In his book, Goldman explains that leaders who develop an "attention" of discerning other's moods, are most effective in their work. Goldman remarks, "The good news is that attention is like a muscle of the mind—we can strengthen our abilities through systematic training."

Exercise this "muscle of the mind" and you will grow in your ability to read people's moods as you meet them and learn what they want in life. Like all skills, the more we practice, the more we improve.

When can you FORM people? Anytime. If I were to meet someone at my son's baseball game, going out to eat, sitting in a coffee shop—am I working? Am I playing? Sure. Both. A unique advantage of network marketing is you have the option of growing a virtual distribution network with the people you meet as you live your life.

I should probably add this: I never bought lists of names to cold-call as a way to grow my business. I realize some successful network marketers do it that way. If you like the idea of cold-calling through long lists of names, that's up to you. The same skills of listening and FORMing still apply.

Finding out what people want and inviting them to look at a solution might sound pretty simple, but it actually is a high-level "people skill." One reason why network marketing companies pay so well for those who build large distribution networks is that very few network marketers take the time to hone these skills to a high level of effectiveness. This is one reason why network marketing can pay as well as what a neurosurgeon earns. Our society pays more for higher skill development.

Once you find out what people want, you can invite them to take a look at your solution. If they say "yes," you tell them about your company. Enter Skill #4.

Skill #1: Be interested in others
Skill #2: Find out what people want
Skill #3: Invite
Skill #4: Present the company story

To "present" simply means to tell a story with a point. You must become "fluent" in sharing your company's story, so that you can communicate it clearly *as it relates to your prospect's need.* Good companies have multiple ways to do this. Some options are CDs, DVDs, online videos, printed material, and live events. Each of these tools has a place. Find out what someone successful in your company does and learn from her. In the process of being mentored, you will eventually figure out your own preference.

My personal style has been to sit down one-on-one in a quiet place like a coffee shop and talk over printed material. Oftentimes, I will follow up an initial meeting by sending an email link to a couple short online videos (two to four minutes each) that they can watch later. I prefer the face-to-face, conversational style of the personal meetings. I like to answer questions in real time. An initial meeting usually takes about an hour.

Whatever format you choose for presenting your company's

story, make sure you can teach it to others. If you're the only one who can present like you do, you won't be able to grow a team. What you do must be able to be duplicated. Keep it simple. You won't create leverage if other people can't duplicate your work. With network marketing, if your team doesn't have success, neither will you.

Once you've shared your company's story, you need to conclude in a way that helps your prospect make a decision. This is called "closing." It makes some network marketers nervous, but it shouldn't.

On to Skill #5: Close and follow up

Skill #1: Be interested in others
Skill #2: Find out what people want
Skill #3: Invite
Skill #4: Present the company story
Skill #5: Close and follow up

A good, one-size-fits-all closing question is, *"So what did you like best about what you heard?"*

Regardless of what they say next, your response should be something like, "Great! Tell me more about that!" You really want to know what *they* like about the solution you just showed them. You want to keep them talking about what they liked because oftentimes the real reason won't come out initially.

Here's an example:

Let's say you just shared your company with Lisa. You sit back in your chair, smile and say, "So tell me, what did you like best about what you just heard?"

Lisa: "I like the pay plan."
You: "Great! Tell me more about that."
Lisa: "I like how you get paid over and over . . . for every time a customer uses the products."
You: "Why do you like that so much?"
Lisa: "Well, I'm killing myself at my job to meet quotas.

It's very stressful. I like how I can grow my income with this new company because, frankly, I want to do something other than work all the time."

I would continue to unpack what, specifically, Lisa doesn't feel like she has enough time for. Her comment about "working all the time" hints at this. Her reason to build a new business will be found in this need she has for more time. I would lead her to imagine and then to *feel* what it would be like to have enough time for the important things in her life.

Keep your prospect talking about what he liked. The more, the better. The "real" reasons usually come out the more you allow the other person to do the talking.

If the person doesn't sign up on the spot, that's okay. But there is something very important you must do next. Before you end your initial meeting, establish a follow-up time to meet again. Don't leave it up in the air. Don't assume one of you will reconnect. That never happens.

It's best if you can follow up within 24–48 hours, because people are *busy*. The longer you wait to follow up, the more likely people will be to forget what they liked about your solution.

To not follow up is to waste the time of all parties involved—yours and your listeners'. Your prospect already invested an hour of her time hearing about your company. You are not bothering her or being pushy when you take the time to follow up. You are giving her the opportunity to think it through and make a decision.

To summarize, the skills you need are:

1. **Be interested in others**
2. **Find out what people want**
3. **Invite**
4. **Present the company story**
5. **Close and follow-up**
6. **Clarify your VISION**

If you treat network marketing seriously, you will develop these skills. If you neglect these skills, you're only kidding yourself. You are exposing a get-rich-quick mentality—whether you realize it or not, you want something for nothing. Obviously, your results will be lackluster at best.

It's no mystery that the marketplace pays for skills. Skills create value for others. This explains why brain surgeons are paid more than fast food workers. Both jobs are needed for society to function, but one requires a lot more skill development than the other. You will serve people with greater effectiveness if you invest in acquiring skills.

Network marketing is an emerging new-economy business model that delivers substantial marketplace value. If you take skill development seriously, you will experience first-hand how a royalty income can dramatically change your life.

One more skill—the "master key."

CHAPTER 8
Skills for Success, Part II

Skill #6 Clarify Your VISION

THE SKILLS EXPLAINED in the previous chapter can equip you to grow a solid business in just five years, *if* you take them seriously. Unless you master each one, your success will be limited. But there is one overarching skill that holds them all together. I call it the "master key." And that skill is clarifying your VISION.

Your VISION is synonymous with your *reason to achieve*. It's your *crystal clear* image of what your future looks like. Living in congruence or in alignment with your deepest values is what your ideal life is all about. Your VISION is a *picture* of what this life looks like. Whatever word you want to use for it, this is the mysterious source of your motivation. And, like the other skills, vision needs to be intentionally *developed*. Let me explain.

The importance of a dream

Once you begin to dream about your future life, something powerful happens. When you dream, you use your imagination. Your imagination creates a picture of the future before it happens. Architects and builders know that every physical structure in existence was created twice—first in the mind, and then in physical form. If it didn't first exist in the mind, it would never manifest in physical form. Mental first, physical second. Your life is the same.

When we dream, we create a powerful awareness at the subconscious level. We actually have two brains, one conscious and one subconscious. Your conscious brain takes care of things you are conscious of—like driving, cooking, reading, and talking. Your subconscious mind takes care of everything else. And unlike your conscious mind that goes to sleep, your subconscious mind never sleeps.

This is why you can remember something "out of the blue" at the strangest times. You wake up in the middle of the night with a great idea. Where did it come from? Your subconscious mind. You ask yourself, "Whom should I invite to the event?" Hours later, when you've forgotten about the event, someone's face pops into your mind. Where did it come from? Yep, your subconscious mind. It never stops working.

This part of our mysterious central nervous system is useful for helping us achieve. Here's why: Our subconscious minds can't distinguish between what is *real* from what is *vividly imagined*. I'll prove it to you: Have you ever cried or been scared at a movie? Your *conscious* mind knows it's only actors saying rehearsed lines on a set, and yet you're crying. Interesting. So how does the subconscious mind help us achieve?

Here's how it works: When you dream about your future life, doing what you love, how does this make you feel? Positively AMAZING!

Guess what happens with amazing energy? It gets translated into productive activity. Just like sunlight can get converted into solar energy and electricity to do work, so our *clear* images of our future can get converted into productive work. Consistent, creative, hard-to-discourage work will grow a profitable business. It could accomplish anything. You are unstoppable.

This is what happens when you imagine a compelling picture of your future life in detail. Your subconscious mind doesn't "get" that it hasn't actually happened yet. Your subconscious mind will act in congruence with what it believes is the current reality. It will solve problems and help you move closer to your dream becoming reality.

Case in point: I'm thinking of several people whom I believe could become good future business partners. The problem is, I hesitate to call them because I don't like rejection. So I stare at my phone and do nothing. Then I remember my dream about my future life, with enough time and money to do the things that really matter to me. I ask myself, "Steve, are you more afraid of hearing another 'no, thanks' or being denied this amazing life?" In other words, what do you fear more—regret or rejection? Will I allow the possibility of hearing 'no, thanks' stand in the way of my dreams? No way. "Give me the phone!"

If giving up on your dream is more painful than the fear of rejection, then you'll work harder to avoid that pain (losing your dream life). Do you see what's happening here? You'll work harder to *avoid* pain than to gain pleasure. If your dream really matters, then the thought of losing it is what causes you the most pain; it's more painful than even the thought of rejection.

So you make those calls and invite your prospects to meet. Your vision of your future life compels you to do the hard work that no one wants to do. Did you catch that? Successful people don't enjoy hard things like rejection, either. *Successful people just do it anyway.* They refuse to let the emotion of fear stand in the way of reaching their goals.

It's well known that "success leaves clues." Always look for the clues.

I have a friend named Jay who had to take his wife to work and then drop off his little boy at daycare. It tore him up to have to separate his family like that. He knew his wife wanted to stay home to raise their child, but they needed the income from her job. Jay used this painful emotion to his advantage. He wouldn't let his fear of rejection deny his wife the joy of being home with their son. Within two years, Jay grew a royalty income business that brought his wife home. Ask me how it feels to watch that happen!

Some people say they don't believe in this "visualization stuff." I get that. Like it or not, we all visualize. We all have a dominant expectation of how we expect our lives to turn out. You can accept the default vision that's been installed into your mental hard drive by a take-the-least-path-of-resistance culture. Or you can intentionally *write your own* vision. Your choice.

Successful people refuse to accept the default vision. Instead, they choose their own dreams carefully. Decades of research show that people with written goals are much more likely to accomplish them. You will also learn from high-achievers that what they wrote down on paper, and sincerely desired to happen, was much more likely to happen.

It's not enough just to "think" your dream. Put it down on paper. Write it out in first person, present tense. You write it out like it is happening today, right now. You describe how it makes you *feel.* Remember how your subconscious mind believes what it sees? Go to a quiet place and give your subconscious mind something amazing to start believing in!

Here's my personal vision statement from 2007.

I don't need an alarm clock to wake up anymore. Can you believe that? I have needed an alarm clock since before I can remember. Now I wake up when I'm done sleeping. I listen to the birds fill the still morning with their song. Wow, does that feel good!

I step outside on the back deck with my coffee and think about the day. The house is quiet.

Today, I will take the boys fishing. It feels amazing to have the time to do something like this during the week! We will stay at our favorite north woods cabin for a few days.

My girls and I are planning our horseback riding trip for next month. I can't wait!

Ever since I replaced my income with a residual income from our business, I work part-time at the hospital. We finally control our calendar! We've never known what it's like to live this way. I feel so free.

For years, the hospital call schedule directed our plans. Now I have enough time for the things that matter most. I feel so satisfied that we are living our lives with intention, and not by default anymore.

And we are blessed to have many friends who are making this journey with us. Watching them come closer to achieving their dreams is more rewarding than words can describe.

We are so thankful for this stage of our lives, for having enough time to capture the little things that we used to miss.

Did you notice how many times I described my *feelings*? That was intentional. It's the feelings which the images create that move a person to action. Just watch what happens in your own life when you do this. Clear images first; feelings second; productive action third.

The mind is powerful. You literally have power to influence your future. The journey won't be easy. You'll make mistakes and probably get hurt. But you'll learn a lot. It's really up to you. What do you want your life to look like in three to five years? It's astonishing that most people will spend more time planning a vacation than they spend planning their lives. Accept that you are 100% responsible for the results. No blaming.

Grab a pad of paper, and go off to a quiet place and dream again. Dream like you did when life was simpler, and when you used to imagine that anything was possible. Use your imagination again. What is burning in your heart to accomplish before your one and only life on this planet is gone? It's a big question.

Do you realize that whatever you accomplish with your life is what you *traded* your life for? Are you satisfied with what you are currently trading your life for?

You must be intentional

One thing I know—no one drifts into a meaningful life. The flow of human nature is to take the path of least resistance. But be warned: If you remain inside your comfort zone, you will die a slow death.

You must be intentional. You must be okay with being unique, even eccentric if need be. Others may misunderstand you, question your motives, even ridicule you. Don't worry about them. Let it go.

Keep your eye on the prize. Keep your vision statement where you can reread it regularly. Hang around like-minded people. Limit your association with negative friends. Be discerning with the words you let take root in your mind. Your mind is like a garden; it must be cultivated carefully or weeds will grow. Be vigilant about which words and ideas you allow in there.

The most influential person Who ever lived is Jesus Christ. Look at what is written about Him as He faced public execution: "Who for the joy set before Him endured the cross." What helped Jesus endure His trial was the joy that was set before him. He focused on the joy, not the trial. The Bible also says that "without vision the people perish." Our vision of the future is an unstoppable force that can fortify us to withstand much difficulty.

I say VISION is a skill because it needs to be developed like the other skills. Defining your vision is more than just *wanting.* We all want. We want more or less of something; we want a better life. We want more free time. We want more money. Wanting is not a skill. It's mental laziness.

Creating a vision statement that emotionally moves you is going to take *work.* You have to *think.* You think about your core values. You think about what really matters to you. You think about what's worth fighting for. That's hard work. Then you put it down on paper, over and over, until the words bring tears to your eyes. Once you've crafted your vision statement in present tense, first person, you have your marching orders. You've created the prize— the prize you will either achieve, or die trying.

Without your vision to aim for, you will grow weary. You will quit. With a clear and compelling vision, nothing will stop you. You may fall down a thousand times, but you won't quit.

Realistic expectations

One last thing to mention in this chapter is not so much a skill as it is a mindset—a mindset shaped by realistic expectations. If you were to be sent out on a journey and warned that there would be a dangerous river to cross in ten miles, then you'd be less likely to panic when you came to the river in ten miles, right? If you know what's coming up ahead, you can mentally prepare. You have informed expectations.

You need to be mentally prepared for something that can be almost intolerably difficult: Much of your work will accomplish nothing long-term for your business. Here's what I mean: When you are out there inviting, presenting, and training, many of the people who get started won't be around in five years. This can be really frustrating.

When I was an electrician years ago, I wired houses. I could look back at the end of the day and see all the work that was completed. The job was done; the wires were in. Thirty years later, I drive by some houses and tell my kids "I wired that house." They roll their eyes. But I did that job well, and the lights are still on today! With network marketing, much of the work you will do is gone five years later. The customers stopped ordering the products. The business partners quit.

The mystery of network marketing is, you won't know who the "won't quit minority" is, so you must *give your best all the time to everyone.*

Now hang on. There is a silver lining here. Even though many of the people you spend time and energy with will not be in your business in five years, you will be paid extremely well on the productivity of those who *do* remain. These lasting business partners are building their *own* businesses. They are finding their *own* customers. They are training their *own* teams. Since you will be likely working with a team where everyone has the same opportunities to grow, you are experiencing real leverage.

To recap, here are the skills:

1. **Be interested in others**
2. **Find out what people want**
3. **Invite**
4. **Present the company story**
5. **Close and follow up**
6. **Clarify your VISION**

These six skills are the foundation for success in network marketing. If you partner with a good company, these skills can change your life in just a few years.

"Strive not to be a success, but rather to be of value."

— Albert Einstein

CHAPTER 9
Our Story—Building a Business Without Losing Friends

ONE OF THE most valuable aspects of life is friendship. Relationships mean everything to us; and they do to you, too. We would not have gone one step with this business if it meant taking advantage of anyone. Nor do we want to lose friends by how we conduct our business.

The good news is, you don't have to lose friends.

Is it possible to be misunderstood at times? Sure. And that's never fun. But this is where your convictions matter. Do you *really* believe you are helping people? It's a personal call to decide whether it's worth being occasionally misunderstood in order to make a difference in the lives of others.

Let me start by saying that unless you understand the work I did *internally*, meaning how I changed my thinking, the external how-to principles won't help you much. If you don't recognize the transformative mental change that is necessary for everyone who succeeds at network marketing, I can predict what will happen—you'll quit.

Here's why: You'll begin the journey and then quickly crash into what seems impossible to you. You'll get discouraged by what you're not good at, or what you don't understand, and you'll conclude that a royalty income business must not be for you. This happens all the time, and I don't want it to happen to you.

Initially, we could not imagine sharing products with anyone. It wasn't until we saw health improvements with our own eyes that we began sharing what we found with others. Don't miss this point: *When we first started, the idea of sharing products with anyone was not even on our radar—but we got started anyway.* Even if you can't imagine talking to anyone, get started *anyway.* It's been said that you don't have to be good to get started; but you *do* have to get started to get good.

Andrea and I were blessed to find a great company right from the beginning. We were both convinced we found something that could help others. We could look people in the eyes and tell them their health would improve if they used our products. You can speak from the heart when you're convinced. And that's a lot more fun than trying to sell.

What will others think?

I need to hit the "pause" button in our story for a moment. I have a confession to make—I had an addiction.

During an early morning prayer walk, I hit a brick wall. When I thought about actually talking to people about my products and company, I started to worry. "What will my colleagues think? What will my friends think? What will they say about me? I'm a doctor. Doctors aren't exactly jumping into network marketing." I was addicted to peer approval, and it paralyzed me.

> And then, an epiphany—I realized I had a choice. I didn't have to *stay* stuck. I could either accept my life the way it was, with time poverty and regret, or I could *decide* that what people think of me doesn't matter all that much.

I sensed God asking me, "Steve, from where are you getting your joy?" To me, the word *joy* means peace, contentment, a sense that all is well with my soul. It's a contentment not dependent upon outward circumstances or other people. It's what we all want. I sensed God asking me where that joy comes from.

I kept walking. Thinking.

My response was, "It comes from You, God. Lasting joy comes from You."

And it was like He challenged me: "If that's really what you believe, then *show* Me you believe it."

Game on.

That was the morning when everything changed for me. From that moment on, I would no longer accept my debilitating addiction to peer approval. I would fight to break free of it.

Take a close look at what you're depending on for joy—circumstances? Peer approval? A good question to ponder is: How much are your fears costing you? Are they worth it?

Addiction to peer approval had been costing me too much. Worrying about what others thought kept me stuck in a predictable pattern of overwork and time poverty. Here's one thing I did about it: I wrote out an affirmation statement, and read it every day for months. It went like this:

> *I believe that joy comes directly from God, from the One who "sees in secret and rewards in secret." Joy doesn't come from what my peers think of me or my circumstances. My joy is secure because it flows from a different Source. My joy and my identity comes from God. My sense of well-being is not contingent upon the whims of what others think of me. I receive joy when I live by faith, when I express gratitude, when I grow personally, and when I give sacrificially.*

Reading these affirmations eventually changed the way I thought. It was like my brain received a software update. When my thoughts changed, everything else began to change. As the saying goes,

> Sow a thought, reap an action.
> Sow an action, reap a habit.
> Sow a habit, reap a character.
> Sow a character, reap a destiny.

And it all started when I *decided* to change the way I think.

Holocaust survivor and neurologist Victor Frankl, Ph.D., relates a profound insight he gained while witnessing the executions of many of his Jewish friends. No matter what the Nazis took away from him, he realized they could never take away this one last thing—his ability to choose.

> Everything can be taken from a man but one thing: the last of the human freedoms—to choose one's attitude in any given set of circumstances, to choose one's own way.
>
> —Viktor E. Frankl, *Man's Search for Meaning*

C. S. Lewis writes that our personal prisons are locked from the *inside.* We could choose to unlock the door and walk out whenever we are ready. Don't allow anyone else to make this choice for you. How awful it would be to get to the end of your life and realize that you let others make the important decisions for you.

I share my personal struggle because we all deal with similar issues. My challenges are not unique. I would hate for anyone not to pursue a royalty income business because you allowed fear of failure or fear of people's opinions to hold you back.

Back to the story. Here's how our business began to grow:

Years one to three

Andrea and I both suffered from arthritic joint pain. We began using our company's products, and in a matter of a few months our pain was essentially gone. As a physician, I was perplexed by this. In medical school I had been taught that vitamins mostly created expensive urine. After spending months researching the topic of nutritional supplementation, I came to realized that there was a dramatic difference in the quality of products offered by various supplement companies. While some companies probably do create "expensive urine" with their products, this was certainly not the case with other science-based, research and development nutritional companies.

When friends would mention health issues, we would recommend a product or two that might help. Oftentimes, they would then set up either a free wholesale account with the company, or join us as business partners. Sometimes they did nothing. Eventually, we started to receive weekly commission checks as more people started to use the products on a regular basis.

Here's how simple our business plan business was: We hosted informal events every couple weeks for people to learn about our company. For the first few years, we met in our home with prospective customers and business partners. We would get the kids to bed by 7:30 PM. I would set up a projector and nail a white sheet over the doorway for a screen. Our "business partners" (mostly old friends) would also invite people to come and learn. Occasionally, we had no-shows. Usually, at least a few folks showed up. I would share our story of how the products had helped us, tell a little about the company, and explain the various ways to get started. We did this over and over in about an hour. Pretty simple stuff.

I'd read somewhere to find a good company and stick with it for at least five years. I knew we'd found a good company. I consciously decided that I wouldn't be like others who jumped from company to company every few years. I studied successful distributors and learned what they did. I listened to their CDs and travelled to hear them speak at events. *I met twentysomething entrepreneurs who earned more royalty income from their distribution networks than I earned as an anesthesiologist!* I became an überstudent.

Network marketing is a mentoring business. It's similar to the mentoring process in medical training. A common saying in medical residency is, "See one; do one; teach one." Seeing, doing, and teaching applies to network marketing also. In the beginning, you need a coach to help you develop skills and learn the business. Then you become a coach and *teach* others.

When meeting with a prospect, I preferred quiet coffee shop settings. When working with new business partners, I would do most of the talking for the first few one-on-one prospecting meetings. Their job was to listen and learn. As time went on, they did more of the talking. Eventually, they became confident and did their own meetings.

Effectively growing your business is about awareness. When you know in your heart that your business and products can make someone's life better, you notice needs that you didn't catch before. It's like when you first buy a new car—it seems so unique, but then, as you start to drive it around town, you start seeing it everywhere!

All I can say is this: If you had asked me *initially* whether I knew even ten people who might want to know about my company, I would have answered "No. No way." I couldn't conceive of walking up to someone and discussing health or financial issues. However, once I benefitted from a first-hand product experience, and I began receiving the residual income checks every week, I started noticing potentially-interested people almost everywhere. Awareness.

My business *modus operandi* was simple: Do something every day to grow my business. Even if all I could manage was to invite someone to our next event or hand out a product catalogue, I did at least one thing every single day to grow my business. *Consistency* may be one of the most powerful words in business.

Limiting Beliefs

We all fight mental battles. We have empowering beliefs and limiting beliefs. To succeed at network marketing, you must delete limiting beliefs and replace them with empowering ones.

Best-selling author Og Mandino helped me replace limiting beliefs with empowering ones. His books suggest affirmation statements to help you reprogram your subconscious mind. Over time, your mind will accept these positive statements as truth. When I understood what Mr. Mandino was doing in his books, I wrote out my own personal affirmation statements to deal with my unique limiting beliefs.

Here's what I wrote:

Affirmation Statements

I am transformed by renewing my mind. (Romans 12)

I lift up my arms with thanks for this priceless gift of a new day.

I walk fast, smile often, and speak loudly.

God is the limitless wellspring of creativity, understanding, wisdom, power, joy, levity and love.

Just as a cold beggar seeks the warmth of a raging bonfire, so I long for His mysterious, transforming presence.

It is His ongoing, redemptive work within me that compels me to grow. His love insists on my maturity.

I continually expand my context (learn new things).

When I take risks, I am not afraid of mistakes. They are some of my best teachers.

I do not waste time or mental energy trying to impress others. Nothing that I truly need comes from what people think of me. God knows what I need, and He alone is able to supply it.

I do not mind being a little eccentric. I am my own person.

I let go caring about what others think of me. Lasting joy will never come from people-pleasing behavior. Joy comes from doing what is right, and from personal growth and maturity.

I continually master new words. Language is a powerful tool that needs to be cultivated.

I will continue to develop leadership skills.

Because I seek win-win, I don't mind confrontation.

I can laugh at myself. Laughter mocks the pride in my life and allows little room for it to grow.

Joy and energy comes not *from others, but from the One Who "sees in secret and rewards in secret."*

Because of confirming past experiences—medical school, residency, speaking and teaching—I know I am well-equipped for the challenges before me.

I am creative, energetic, visionary, resourceful, and have a bias for action.

I am blessed with strong people skills; I have an uncommonly good memory; and I have a knack for identifying the heart of a matter.

I will live this day as though it is my last. And if it is not, I shall fall to my knees and give thanks.

The above statements probably seem odd to you. They are very personal and unique to my own challenges. I read them every morning for months, and my life changed. Do whatever it takes to replace limiting beliefs with empowering ones. Use Og Mandino's books, or write out your own.

Years three to five

These were the years our business really took off. Going part-time in my anesthesia practice opened up a couple days each week to meet with prospects. I tried to schedule two or three business meetings every day I had off.

I cannot stress enough the importance of attending every big event that your company offers. Andrea and I attended our company's international conventions annually. These gatherings are where belief and vision and relationships are solidified. Don't underestimate the power of a room filled with like-minded people who share a common vision. Mental synergy is powerful beyond description. Some of the most important dreams for my future took shape while attending events. *Do everything you can to get your business partners to attend big events!*

I met my mentors at events. I heard Dean speak from stage and knew I needed to meet him. Dean is an attorney who replaced his lucrative law practice income with a royalty income business. He became one of my closest friends. Even though I wasn't a part of his business network, he generously shared hours of his time with me. I am grateful for his wise counsel. (Not too often does a doctor say that about an attorney!)

In order to stay connected to my team, I sent out a weekly email promoting upcoming events and conference calls. I honored people who were advancing in their businesses. I would share specifically what I was learning and what I was doing to build my business. Find out the preferred communication style for your business partners. A private team Facebook page has also been invaluable for creating a sense of community, especially when the business network spread across the country.

While driving, I was constantly listening to educational CDs. I collected a large CD library that has helped me immensely. I recommend you do the same. Jim Rohn, Tony Robbins, *Success Maga-*

zine's Darren Hardy, Tim Sales, Robert Kiyosaki, Paul Zane Pilzer, Artemis Limpert, Richard Brooke, John Maxwell, Zig Ziglar, and Brian Tracy are some of my favorites. Your company may provide educational CDs or podcasts. Make your car a classroom on wheels: "Mobile University" is a great use of otherwise wasted time.

Eventually I began creating my own training content. I would invite our team to our home to study various topics like *Finding Customers, Crafting a Vision Statement, Product Overview* and *Handling Objections.* Our team did book studies. We learned and grew and ate good food and had fun together.

Income-producing *versus* non-incoming-producing work

It's important to know the difference between income-producing and non-income-producing activity.

Examples of income-producing tasks include meeting new people, FORMing, inviting, presenting, and training. Non-income-producing work would include cleaning your office, creating a vision statement, and reading. See the difference? The latter has a legitimate place, but be aware of the tendency to resist income-generating activity. Why do we avoid it? We avoid it because it involves the fear of rejection. Non-income-generating activity is easier since it provokes no rejection.

Don't deceive yourself into thinking you are doing lots of hard work if most of it is non-income-generating work. What's harder to do: Watch your company's online videos or pick up the phone and invite someone to meet? Which activity might elicit rejection? Which one will grow your business?

If my team members tell me they are working their business ten hours a week and they have no presentations that week, I know they are spending most of their time doing non-income-generating activity. People will even fool themselves into *thinking* they are working the business when they aren't. Why do they do this? Sometimes they don't know *what* to do. A mentor can help address this. Everyone who is serious about their game has an accountability coach. We all work harder for a coach than we will for ourselves.

As a rule of thumb, you want to spend 80% of your time with

income-generating work, and only 20% of your time with non-income-generating work. The reasons should be obvious.

Years five to seven

I'm a first-generation, eastern European immigrant from a single-parent, blue-collar family. In my garage, there is a three by four foot old wooden crate that my grandfather built. It contained all of my grandparent's worldly possessions when they came to America in 1951. And now here I am, the owner of a life-changing, royalty-income business. There is a verse in the Bible that says, "To whom much is given, much is required." I have been given much, and I want to exercise wise stewardship over everything—money *and* time.

Shortly after leaving my full-time anesthesia practice, a horrific earthquake destroyed Port-au-Prince, Haiti. That night, I received an email asking for help. Doctors—especially anesthesiologists—were needed at a make-shift field hospital run by a Christian adoption agency. How could I *not* help? God blessed me with time freedom. How could I just sit back and enjoy it all when I was *available* to go?

A couple days later, I was on a jet to Haiti with a team of volunteer medical providers. We did what we could to amputate crushed limbs, sew up lacerations, pull maggots from wounds, even deliver a baby in the middle of the night without electricity. We used a generator, construction lamps, and a picnic table as our operating room. We delivered a healthy baby girl to a mom who was hemorrhaging.

While many of my medical colleagues wished they could have responded, because of time constraints, they were unable to help. They couldn't get the time off from work. That was when the incredible power of royalty income really hit me in full force. *Because of the recurring income stream from my distribution network, I had the freedom to go.*

Royalty income brings freedom

Because of royalty income, I could literally leave the country with only a moment's notice. I had no payroll or inventory to deal with, no debt to manage and no account receivables to wait for. I owned a virtual distribution network that was flowing with millions of dollars' worth of high-quality, high-demand, consumable nutritional products.

Since my customers received the best price with the automatic monthly reorder program, most of the product orders were automated. The company collected all payments, and deposited my commission check electronically each week. I have received that weekly check—every single week—for over eight years now!

As a result, I could literally leave the country for an indefinite length of time without creating the slightest hiccup in my business. There would be no mountain of paperwork to plow through or fires to extinguish when I returned. Can you think of any other business like this?

It seemed almost to good to be true, and yet it happened! *And it's happening for thousands of people all around the world who are growing a non-traditional, direct-to-consumer, distribution network instead of a traditional bricks-and-mortar, employee-based business.*

How to build your business without losing friends

A friend told me that he would never get into network marketing because he likes having friends. Sadly, some people feel this way because of bad past experiences.

The truth is, you *don't* have to lose friends. Remember when we discussed the FORM process? This is where you genuinely want to find out what's important to others. If you really listen to people, you'll find needs. And you'll be able to honor people in the process.

If you genuinely believe that your product will make someone's life better, and someone is struggling in that very area, why would you *not* share what you have? Isn't that the *right* thing to do? Personally, I felt I had an ethical responsibility to share what I had.

This is why heartfelt conviction is essential. When you're convinced, you can speak from the heart. You won't feel like you're selling. If you are *not* convinced, then you'll feel conflicted inside. You'll have mental noise to deal with. Mental distractions like, "What if she thinks I'm doing this only to make a sale?" Thoughts like this originate from a win-lose nagging feeling in your heart.

In order to feel win-win, you will need two things:

1. A clear understanding about what people's needs are (because you *really* listened to them).
2. A belief that you can help them.

Once you possess these two things, you'll always feel win-win about the transaction. No mental noise. No internal conflict. Just a quiet satisfaction that you helped someone and grew your business at the same time.

Finally, one last thing. Once you mention your solution, and they get what it is you're offering, you must be willing to let it go. You must not keep bringing it up over and over. After they've considered what you offered, and you've asked them if they'd like to try it—if they decline, you must drop it. Answer any questions and misunderstandings, yes. But once they understand what it is, let it go.

Your ability to walk away takes a disciplined mindset; you must remain emotionally detached from the outcome. If you continue to mention your solution, you will risk hurting the relationship. If you bring the same topic up every time you get together, they will avoid you. Do NOT let this happen. If you *won't get off it*, you *will* lose friends.

People give network marketing a bad reputation because they don't know when to let it go. Don't chase people. Don't flood their email inboxes with your stuff. Don't put a marketing pamphlet in front of them every time you're together. Be okay with hearing "no" for an answer. Certainly keep the door open, but mentally move on.

If you learn to do this, you will help many of your friends and family, and they won't feel put off by your approach. If you've done a good job listening to them, sharing your solution, answering their questions, and asking if they want to give it a try—then you've done your job! You have served them well.

If you follow the above guidelines, you *won't* lose friends as you build your business. We've had the joy of watching many of our family and friends benefit from our products and business. We also have friends who *don't participate*. And that's okay. The Golden Rule is a good guideline here: Treat others like you want to be treated. It's hard to go wrong with the Golden Rule.

CHAPTER 10
Common Objections

IF YOU ARE thinking this through for the first time, you likely have some questions. Here are four of the most common.

1. Is network marketing a "pyramid scheme"?

When people ask this question, they usually mean one of two things:

a. Is it illegal or unethical?
b. Isn't it inherently *unfair* because only the ones who get in early make good money?

Let's begin with the question of legality first. The Federal Trade Commission may consider a business model *illegal* if you get paid without helping to move products or services from the company to the consumer. In other words, if you are getting paid for no reason other than signing people up, then you may be engaged in an illegal business.

Conversely, if you are getting paid *a percentage of sales generated* from the flow of products or services in your distribution network, then it is much more likely that the business you are a part of is legal.

Ponzi Scheme

Another name for a pyramid scheme is a "Ponzi scheme," named after Charles Ponzi, who made it infamous in the 1920s. A "Ponzi scheme" refers to a pseudo-business model where investors give their money with promises of higher-than-normal returns on their investment. The money they get back (or *don't* get back) from their "investment" does not come from anything actually increasing in value. Their "investment return" actually comes from subsequent investors who put their money into the scheme. The earlier investors receive some of the money paid into the system from subsequent investors.

A Ponzi scheme is totally dependent on people continuing to inject new money into the system. (Not unlike the American Social Security System, which could be considered the largest "*legal* Ponzi scheme" in history.)

Fraudulent companies have tried to conduct business like this under the guise of legitimate network marketing companies. Learn to recognize that a pyramid scheme is dependent on new people constantly buying into the system. Since there is no real value being created or real products being delivered to customers, investment returns or commissions can come only from fresh money being injected into the bogus pyramiding scheme.

By contrast, with a legitimate network marketing company, you are paid from the sales of products or services that flow to customers *via* a distribution network. Even with no new people joining your organization, you could continue earning a commission for years. Why? Because you are being paid from the sales of products that continually flow from the company to satisfied customers, month after month after month. Granted, if no new customers are found, the company is not likely to *grow*, but it can still be a profitable company. And you can still earn a residual income for years without adding new customers.

Think of it like this: From this moment on, if no new customers ever tried Starbucks, but all the previous customers who like Starbucks coffee continue to buy Starbucks, won't the company and its thousands of employees continue to get paid? As long as coffee flows through the local stores, the company will continue to generate millions of dollars in sales—*even if Starbucks were never to gain another customer.*

Always ask: Are products or services flowing to customers? The answer to this question will safeguard you from being a part of anything illegal. The continual flow of products is a distinguishing mark of legitimacy for any company, traditional or non-traditional. I hope this helps to answer the "is it legal?" concern.

Now lets answer the "Is it fair?" question:

Some people think that only the distributors who get in early, who are already at the top, are the ones who make any money. Given the triangular shape of a distribution network, it is understandable that someone might think this way.

Let me ask a question. What business do you know of where people at the *bottom* make more money than the people at the *top*? Or what business pays workers who have *less* experience than it pays workers with *more* experience? Would it be a good business if "entry level" associates made more money than the executives who've already worked their way up?

To illustrate how network marketing's business structure compares with a traditional company, please see the triangle diagram below.

The Corporate Pyramid

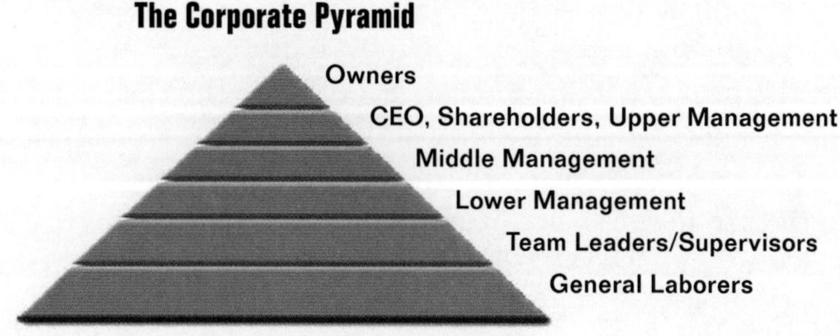

Does your company have a CEO, a president, vice president, middle management and support staff? Why does the CEO earn more than the employees? The higher up you rise in the corporate structure, the more value you are expected to add to the organization, and the more responsibility you bear. Of course, as we mentioned when explaining the concept of leveraging OPT, the CEO is paid on the productivity of everyone else in the organization.

I enrolled a young man named Jordan into my business a couple years after I started, so he is below me in the distribution network. He is smart, very disciplined, and a hard worker. Today, he has personally enrolled more business partners and customers than I have. As a result he earns more money than I do. What do you call that? I call it *fair!*

Through the team he has built, Jordan serves hundreds of customers each month. While every network marketing company pay plan differs, in our company, Jordan earns more money than I do—*even though I got started a couple years before him.*

Paid for what you produce

I make about the same income as the very first person who signed up with my company—even though he got started *fifteen years* before me. How can that be possible? With our particular company, we are not paid for our seniority. We are paid only for the products that flow through the distribution network we helped to build. There may not be a more fair compensation system on the planet.

As far as the triangular shape goes, what organizational structure *doesn't* have that shape? Can you think of one? The government does; your family tree does; your church does; every corporation does; the military does; the Boy Scouts do. The shape merely represents a logical chain of command. Think of architecture. It's the same principle: The base that supports the building is always larger than the top of the structure. It's simply logical.

I hope this helps with the "is network marketing fair/is it legal?" question.

2. I can't sell

"I can't sell" is a roadblock that prevents many people from even considering network marketing. The word "sharing" better describes what we really do. We share solutions with people who are "solution-oriented."

Once you engage the process, here's what might happen:

> First, you begin personally using the products or service.
>
> Second, you determine whether that product or service is benefiting you. Does it make your life better? Does it provide a solution to some problem or concern you have?
>
> Third, if you answered "yes" to the above question, you then decide if the product is fairly priced.

A few months after I began using my nutritional products, my annoying shoulder pain went away. No steroid shots. No long-term NSAID use. No side-effects. My wife also had a similar product experience with her hand pain. She had been receiving steroid shots in her finger joints to relieve the pain. Her pain was also now gone—with no more shots!

We were convinced. Do you see how the mindset change began to occur at this point for Andrea and me? When you are convinced that you've found something that helps you, and you see someone suffering from the same problem, what do you do about that? Do you remain silent? Do you watch your friend suffer and say, "Oh, that's unfortunate"? Or do you try to help? Most of us want to help.

Here's what changes: When we genuinely believe in our hearts that we've found something that can help others, most of us will want to share that information. Just like you would tell others about a good movie or restaurant or babysitter. (We've actually learned *to stay quiet* about our babysitters, because then they aren't available for us!)

The "I can't sell" feeling usually stems from doubt that the product or service really works. When you feel like you are only selling, you feel win-lose about it. You win; your friends lose. A win-lose deal bothers most good people. It should!

When you have the conviction that your product or service can really improve the lives of others, you will share from the heart. Speaking from the heart is more fun than using clever sales lines.

Ok, I can hear you thinking, "Yeah, but I'm not getting *paid* to share the movie or restaurant or babysitter. I feel weird sharing something and getting *paid* for it. What if my friends think that's *why* I'm sharing it? What if they think I'm doing it solely to make a buck?"

I wrestled with mental noise for a long time. "What if my friends think I'm using my doctor credentials and wellness products to make money off them?" That question really bothered me for a long while.

Until one memorable day. A nurse with whom I was working also had some experience in network marketing. I was telling her how conflicted I felt about sharing my products and getting paid, she wisely asked me,

> "Dr. Hryszczuk, when you give someone anesthesia, do you get paid?"
>
> "Of course," I replied.
>
> "Then what's the difference?"

Wham! I got it!

Economics 101

It's morally appropriate to get paid when we create value for someone. This is how the marketplace works. Good business is always win-win. Good business makes people's lives better.

If you make the effort to find out what people want, take the time to learn about your products, and then make recommendations for someone who has a need—why *shouldn't* you get paid for that? You would be functioning as a consultant. You've invested both time and energy to gain specialized product knowledge. If that's your business, then why *wouldn't* adding value like that deserve compensation in return? We financially compensate the workers who change our oil, cut our hair, and fix our computers.

So when someone says, "I can't sell," what that usually means is, "I'm not convinced yet. I feel like I would be doing it just for the money. I won't do this to my friends." These are the sentiments of an honest person, an honest person *not yet convinced.*

I always reassure new business partners not to worry about promoting the products until they convince themselves. I deliberately use those words "Convince *yourself*"–***not*** "I'll convince you."

Personal Conviction

Traditional sales is sometimes called "B2B sales." This is *business to business* sales, where you represent your company to another company. Network marketing is different. I call it "P2P," *person to person* sales. P2P is vastly different from B2B sales. P2P sales requires heartfelt conviction that what you are promoting truly can help another person.

You must feel *that* convinced, because network marketing is marketing to *your* network, *your* relationships. Sharing with people in your personal network without feeling conflicted requires personal conviction.

Some successful B2B sales reps can't handle network marketing because they take the rejection personally. *Person to person* marketing feels more personal than *business to business for an important reason*—because it *is*! A real live human being whom you know and maybe even respect is looking you in the eye and answering you with either a "yes, please" or a "no, thanks." How can that *not* feel personal?

In summary, the objection "I can't sell" usually comes from a lack of belief in the effectiveness of your product or service. First, convince yourself that your products work and are fairly priced. Then, understand that it's absolutely right to be compensated as a consultant who makes people's lives better.

Two more objections to go.

3. I don't have enough time.

Successful people are busy. How could someone with a full-time job and a family find the time to grow a part-time business? It's a valid concern.

First of all, nothing in your life will ever change until you create some new patterns. New patterns lead to new results. If you're content with your *status quo*, then—don't change anything. Stay the same. Ten years from now your life will look the same as it does now. If you're okay with that, great. Don't figure it out. But since you're reading this book, my guess is you're probably *not* okay with the way things are.

Do you lack the time to do the things you used to dream about? Travel? Adventures with your family or friends? Time to learn something new? Time to care for an aging parent? Time to be more involved at your kids' school or church or civic events? Or what about time to enjoy a hobby or just relax?

If you want to gain back more time, you must solve an ancient riddle: You must find a way to generate income without selling your limited time to do it. Many would say this is impossible. But it *is* possible. For most of us, it will require a significant paradigm shift.

I like Robert Kiyosaki's definition of an asset *vs.* a liability: An *asset* is something that puts money in your pocket. A *liability* is something that takes money out of your pocket.

Most of us have plenty of liabilities and zero assets. An asset is something that pays you without even requiring you to show up. Your job isn't an asset. If you don't show up, do you still get paid? No. Your home isn't an asset—if you lose your job, does your home put money into your pocket? No. It takes money out. Positive cash flow from real estate is an asset. Owning a franchise is an asset. Owning a distribution network of consumable products is an asset.

People who sacrifice time now to build assets will find they have more time later in life. In that sense, it's not so much a sacrifice as it is an investment. You are choosing to put your time into something now so that you can reap exponentially greater time dividends later.

Think about what it would feel like to have an additional income stream of several thousand dollars per month. What would it feel like to replace half or all of your "day job" income? What would it feel like to have every Friday off? What would your life look like if you could work part-time?

The realization that we don't have enough time can be a powerful motivation to build an asset. It all starts with desire. "When the student is ready, the teacher arrives." It's probably not a coincidence that you're reading a book like this right now. . . .

If we are honest with ourselves, most of us could admit we have discretionary or wasted time each week. How many hours each week do we watch TV, look at Facebook or engage in a hobby? If we are really serious about creating positive changes, most of us could come up with at least ten hours each week to work a new business.

So, if you don't have enough time to launch a low-risk royalty income business, are you okay with that fact? Are you content with the direction your life is headed when it comes to the precious commodity of *your* time? If you don't like where you are, or the direction you are headed, you can change this if you choose.

4. I don't have enough money to get started.

It's important to acknowledge that some people truly have been hit by a financial storm—family disruptions, health emergencies, and job terminations can leave people financially devastated. Poor timing to launch a new business due to lack of finances can be a very real factor.

For most others however, their claim to not have the money to get started can often be tracked back to a chronic problem—poor spending habits. Too many people buy into the easy credit and consumption culture. They think that they cannot possibly survive without cable TV, daily expensive coffee drinks, fast food, and yet another pair of shoes. Parkinson's Law unfortunately rings true too often: "A luxury, once enjoyed, becomes a necessity."

If this is you, be brutally honest with yourself. Make a decision to part company with *status-quo* thinking. Your current assumptions about what you think you need in order to feel or look successful has you financially stuck. Decide today to embrace new ideas, *better* ideas, about the dollars flowing through your hands.

Ideas always precede action; consistent action can change your life—it all starts with *how you think about things.* I know of people who sold a couch or TV set to get started in business, and today they have a growing distribution network!

Study people you admire who have already done what you want to accomplish. Learn how they *think differently* than you. Unpack their ideas about money, work, business and abundance. Then, expose how you think about those same topics. Make a thorough comparison so you are crystal clear on the differences. Let go of your ego here. If their way of thinking differs from your way of thinking, YOU are the one who should change.

If we change the way we think, we can change our reality. Outward change is always an inside job. You can begin your own transformation process today. Ask a high achiever which books influenced them the most. What a great question to ask a successful person! Set aside 30 minutes a day to read and think and expand your reality. "The more that you read, the more things you will know. The more that you learn, the more places you'll go," says Dr. Seuss.

If you've been making poor financial decisions, don't let a lack of money stop you. Make a budget. Start saving. Get creative. Ask for help. Cut out all the nonessential expenses and reinvest the same dollars into your own personal development account. Investing in yourself is the best investment to make.

Getting past objections

Most objections are related to one of those four we've named—It's a pyramid scheme; I can't sell; I don't have enough time; I don't have enough money. If you know it's time to make a change, work through your roadblocks. Please realize this: Imagine how much it could be costing you—financial and otherwise—if you decide just to stay stuck.

Growing a virtual distribution network of high-demand, consumable products is the most accessible way to build your very own royalty income business. Robert Kiyosaki puts it best with the title of his book on network marketing. He calls it *The Business of the 21st Century*. I couldn't agree more.

> It is always strange and painful to have to change a habit of mind; though, when we have made the effort, we may find a great relief, even a sense of adventure and delight, in getting rid of the false and returning to the true.
>
> —Dorothy Sayers, *Why Work?*

CHAPTER 11

What Say You?

SINCE YOU'VE MADE it this far, you're likely serious about creating positive changes in your life. Congratulations! Maybe you are sick of not having enough time for important things in life. Maybe you know you have more potential with which to serve humanity and you're current employment is not allowing you to develop it. Maybe you are not adequately financially compensated for the value you bring to the marketplace.

Whatever your reason, you need a new plan. And it's time to work *smarter*, not just harder. You know one thing for sure—you were put on Earth to do more with your life than what you're currently doing. You know this is true, but you've never had a plan before . . . until now.

Please allow me to be direct: If you partner with a good company, and begin this journey with a teachable, going-back-to-school-mentality, you can build a life-changing royalty income business within five years. It will be one of the more challenging things you do in life; but if you apply the foundational business principles and skills described here, you can succeed—like so many others have before you.

Network marketing has so many advantages. *You* get to decide who works with you. You decide *when* you want to work. You decide *where* in the world you want to work. You decide the culture of your team. You decide how quickly you want to grow your business. You decide the product line or service you want to represent, and how to market it. It is customized entrepreneurship at its finest.

Network marketing puts you in the driver's seat. You make the decisions, and then you accept full responsibility. Do you like the thought of being the CEO of your own enterprise? What about one day being a mentor and showing others how to succeed? Imagine the satisfaction of knowing you are serving hundreds of satisfied customers *via* the combined efforts of your team.

What other business opportunity can offer advantages that come even close to the advantages of a network marketing business? What other low-risk business model give you the opportunity of owning a virtual distribution network of high-demand, consumable products, producing a residual, leveraged and tax-advantaged income stream? If another such opportunity exists outside of network marketing, I am not aware of it.

What will your life look like?

So the question you need to ask yourself is: *What do I want my life to look like in five years?*

What income do you want?
How much free time would you like?
What kind of home do you want to live in?
What car do you want to be driving?
What experiences do you want your kids to have?
What causes do you want to support?
What memories do you want to create with the people you love?
How physically healthy do you want to be?
How much debt do you want to have, or *not* have?
How much influence do you want in others' lives?

The final answers to these questions are completely up to you.

Remember, we're talking about your one-and-only life. Too often I see people passively accept the limiting beliefs of their peers. Why let someone else tell you how much vacation time you can take? Why let someone else decide what's possible for you? Why let someone else write the script for your life?

If you want to know what your life will look like in five years, I can tell you: Look around at your friends. The people with whom you spend the most time have a profound influence on your thinking. It's said that our income will be an average of the incomes of our five closest friends. Of course, money is not the only, nor even the most important, criterion for friendship. But maybe it's time to *limit* your exposure to someone who opposes rather than supports your goals. Maybe it's time to make some *new* friends.

The choice is yours

Maybe up until now you've lacked a track to run on. If your current employment doesn't allow you to develop your strengths and address your weaknesses, network marketing will. You will grow more than you ever imagined. Growth is liberating. You feel alive when you are growing personally. Your business will grow as much as you grow. That's why people who take shortcuts always end up quitting.

Why are you frustrated in your current situation? I'll tell you why. It's because you've settled. You've believed the lie that your dreams are unobtainable. Then you validated your excuses by looking at what everyone else was doing. Your friends don't speak of beautiful dreams that they are fighting for. You neglected your dreams, and over time they faded out. We pay a personal price when we let a vision die like that. Something dies inside of us, too.

Can you recall how you felt the last time you attempted something really hard, something that even scared you, and you succeeded? Remember how exhilarating it was? There's nothing like that feeling! That's the kind of life we were meant to live. The process of learning and growing and overcoming develops our potential and increases our ability to serve and impact others. It creates a positive upward spiral.

Maybe you've been spiraling downward. Taking the path of least resistance is easier, but it's not for you. You were made for more.

Reach out to the person who gave you this book. Ask him or her to sit down and talk with you about these ideas. Examine that person's company with objectivity. You know how to evaluate a business now. Think it through for yourself.

It's been said that we attract success by the people we become. I can promise you this—regardless of how much money you make, the person you become as a result of this journey will be the best thing that happens to you. Money just makes us more of what we already are. Becoming a better listener, a more effective communicator, unafraid of what others think of us—what's the value of this?

The next five years will fly by regardless of what you decide to do about your financial future. Why not welcome the life of your dreams, starting now! How incredible would that be? It could happen, you know. "The journey of a thousand miles begins with one step." Take the next step. You have a vision that excites you for a reason. It's no accident that these dreams have been placed in your heart. You have tremendous, untapped potential waiting to be developed. Now, use this knowledge you've gained, and get to work. Your future is waiting for you.

CHAPTER 12
A Word from Others Who Have Made the Journey

TO GIVE YOU a more complete look at how this industry can change lives, I asked other network marketing leaders to share their "before and after" story. These are real people who were kind enough to share their age and occupation when they got started.

Leanne Jacobs, 29, Sales Manager

What was hard about my life before was my schedule, and an overall feeling of always rushing and being behind. I didn't feel free in any way. I was completely stressed and misaligned with my core values. I was burning out mentally and physically, and was chasing ambition (but lacking fulfillment). Work consumed my life. Because everyone around me was in the same boat, it became a sort of normal state to be stressed, overwhelmed and 'busy being broke'. Although I had a great salary, I always struggled to fast-track my finances. After paying my mortgage and bills each month, I had a little left for savings and wasn't really getting ahead at a pace I was happy with. I also didn't feel I was contributing to the world to a level that I knew I was capable of.

What is better since growing my business: Everything! I am completely in control of my schedule and my day. I get to choose what I want to do and when. I have since had the time, energy and clarity in my life to fill it with my fabulous husband and 4 children. I spend my days exactly how I want to. I have also integrated my business with my family so we do things as a team. Our children share in our business success. We have the freedom to pursue what we love and spend our time together.

I feel so blessed in every way that I have a lifestyle that most people desire but haven't been taught how to formulate. Network marketing allows people to align with an industry and company that aligns best with them. For me, this meant aligning with a wellness company. I am so passionate about wellbeing and how critical it is to make nutrition a family priority. Every day, I am paid to do what I love: mentor individuals who desire a more fulfilling and abundant life as well as help heal the world through nutrition. I am grateful every day.

Collette Larsen, 42, Stay-at-home mom with occasional part-time jobs

In 1994 I was a single, stay-at-home mother with a high school education, very limited business experience and five children to support. A difficult divorce and sky-rocketing medical bills had left me financially and emotionally devastated. I was facing bankruptcy, the likelihood of losing our home and also struggling to cope with the needs of my two youngest daughters who had been born with Cystic Fibrosis—a chronic degenerative disease. I needed to be at home to provide round-the-clock care for my youngest daughter who had just undergone a double-lung transplant and somehow support my other four children at the same time. My family's future was sitting squarely on my shoulders and I was desperate.

Looking back on my situation, it seems the timing to start a business could not have been worse. I've since learned that most opportunities come at inopportune times, so they are often misinterpreted as distractions! I started my network marketing business with the lofty goal of making enough income to simply pay for the nutritional products I needed for my family. Within a few months I realized my business might also provide the means to put food on the table and pay the most pressing of our bills. As my understanding of where this profession could take me expanded, I set a goal to prevent bankruptcy and to dig myself out of debt. As the months and years passed, my vision grew and possibilities became realities.

Fast forward 20 years:

Today, I have achieved complete financial and time freedom. My humble home-based business has evolved into an international family enterprise with my grown sons as my partners. We now have the ability to go anywhere we want and in fact, we have traveled the world as a family. I work and play with people who lift me, people I respect and admire. I live a dream-come-true life, spending my time with my husband, children and 15 grandchildren doing exactly what I love to do—making priceless memories. My husband and I now divide our time between our home in San Diego and a cottage on Lake Tahoe.

Brian Bohlke, 23, Personal banker with Wells Fargo

I was a recent college graduate still trying to find my way in my new journey after college. Getting a job was the only option I knew; it's just what you do after college. Money was tight. I graduated with $16,000 in credit card debt, so I was starting off my life digging out of a hole. At 23 years-old, with no experience in corporate America, my income at my job was small, barely enough to pay bills and eat. I lived in a two-bedroom apartment with a roommate. And that is where my life sat. I literally was already bored after only 18 months of working! I couldn't believe how much I did not like going to work, but what other option did I have?

After being introduced to network marketing, I have to say the first thing that changed was my mindset. I was challenged to read. Those first two books changed the course of my life, because they changed the way I thought about money. Having a paradigm shift in your life is far more impactful than just accumulating more information. I am now 36 years-old, married to the love of my life, have two beautiful children. What's more, I have been "unemployed" for 8 years! Network marketing gave me more options. Plain and simple, it offered me something other than a routine job. It gave me the ability to grow at my pace, earn at my pace, and decide what my future would look like. I thank God daily for the introduction to this industry.

J Leman, 27, Retired professional football player

Although I was living my dream of becoming a professional football player, it was not all bliss. I had no job security: I was cut from the team (fired!) 7 times in 4 years. This led me to many different cities for short periods of time and never being able to put down roots. Because of this, I rarely got to see my wife during the season. And spending time with family is a high priority for me. Worse yet, I ended up compromising my health playing football. The accumulation of injuries eventually forced me to retire. A persistent friend convinced me to sit down and take an objective look at a business opportunity I only mocked in the past.

Today, because of our network marketing business, my life is vastly different. I usually eat all three meals a day with my kids, and go on an evening walk with my whole family. My wife is able to be a full-time stay-at-home mom, which was her dream. I have more free time, better health, and more income now than I did as a professional football player.

Steven Solverson, 54, Metallurgical Laboratory Technician

Before our network marketing business I worked long hours, was rarely home and always tired. We always traded our time for money.

Now, I feel better health-wise than when I was in my thirties, and have met many nice people along the way. We have been able to create a leveraged income that can even be willed to our children. Believe me when I say, retirement is a lot nicer when you get a "social security" check every week instead of once a month.

Maureen Solverson, 51, Sales advisor for a promotional company

Before partnering with our wellness company, I was getting sick all the time and had shingles twice. I wanted to get my health back.

My health is much better now, and I enjoy all the positive personal growth that comes with the network marketing experience. Being with a group of like-minded people all moving towards a common goal has been so rewarding. It has been beneficial to my health, finances and relationships. I love that this journey has grown me from the inside out and helped me dream again, and dream bigger. Because of this business, I am becoming the leader that God wants me to be.

Gene Onley, 51, Small business owner

As a business owner, the buck always stopped with me. With three offices, and sales and service personnel in each location, it should have been the dream career. The real truth was—the hours and the pressure were taking a toll on my health.

I was totally shocked one day when they rushed me to the hospital with coronary artery disease. I was in and out of the hospital for the next 18 months. My business took a real hit, and I ended up selling it. I lost 60 pounds and struggled with hopelessness. My wife decided there had to be a better way, and she started researching what God would have us do to get my health back.

We tried nutritional products from over two dozen different companies. We learned in the process that very few products had any kind of potency or quality guarantee. There were a handful that were "pharmaceutical grade," so that became the standard we used to select our supplements. This led us to the network marketing company we would partner with.

Once I got my health back, we couldn't stop sharing our story with others. Today, we have a very nice residual income business—without the stress and pressures of employees, inventory and overhead costs. I am now in my mid 70's, and grateful for the ongoing income from our business. Now we can enjoy our kids, grandkids and great grandkids that God has blessed us with.

Eric Martindale, 29, Carpenter and personal trainer

After finishing my Masters Degree in 2010 I found myself at a fork in the road: Do I jump into the work force like everyone else or do I choose a path less traveled? To answer this question, I looked at the traditional route of "work 40 hours per week for the next 40 years" (The 40-40 Plan). For someone like myself who loves traveling, climbing, skiing, surfing and many other activities, the 40-40 Plan made me cringe. I didn't have a clue what I was going to do, I just knew I didn't want the traditional route. For the first two years after graduate school I did carpentry, landscaping and personal training to pay the bills. All were decent paying jobs, but I was always trading my time for money and the only opportunity I had to "get ahead" was to increase the amount of hours I worked. It got to the point where I was working 12-14 hours per day, six or seven days a week!

I was introduced to network marketing in 2012, and my life has never been the same. Not only has entrepreneurship given me the opportunity to create complete freedom in my life, it is a gift I get to share with others. I now get joy helping others achieve their own freedom. This business is called the "economy equalizer" because it doesn't matter what your age, sex, ethnicity, education or background is; if you're teachable, motivated and have a willingness to work you can create the life of your dreams. The friendships I've formed, the personal growth I've experienced, and the positive environment of like-minded individuals who support and inspire me to live my dreams are the hidden treasures I have found in network marketing.

Jordan Kemper, 22, Student

Since childhood, my dream was to become a medical doctor. I was fascinated with the human body, and loved helping people. After an internship during my last year in college, I was so dismayed to see the direction that the medical field was going. More than half of the physicians I shadowed told me to strongly consider something other than medicine. Disappointed and discouraged, I wasn't sure what I would do after college. I wanted to be a difference maker in this life, but my vision was cloudy.

I agreed to take a look at a network marketing opportunity solely because a medical doctor told me it was worth considering. After 45 minutes with Dr. Steve Hryszczuk at a tiny coffee shop, I felt hope once again in my life.

I had zero business experience, but massive amounts of passion. It took me about 18 months of struggling in this industry before I realized that people were my product. As my people skills improved, I began to see more and more success. I've been a proud member of just one company for 8 years, and earned more than $2 million in commissions. I just recently got married, and my dream of financial freedom for my family is now a reality.

I've traveled to more than 15 countries to inspire people worldwide. My organization includes more than 4,000 customers and distributors. Each person I meet has a story that matters to me, and I find so much joy in using the network marketing industry to enhance their quality of life. Day after day, my legacy grows not by the dollars that I make, but by the lives that I touch. I am so thankful that someone took the time to share this opportunity with me.

Suggested Reading

The Next Millionaires by Paul Zane Pilzer

Thou Shall Prosper by Rabbi Daniel Lapin

Rich Dad Poor Dad by Robert Kiyosaki

Cash Flow Quadrant by Robert Kiyosaki

Business for the Glory of God by Wayne Grudem

The 21 Irrefutable Laws of Leadership by John Maxwell

Every Good Endeavor by Tim Keller

The Business of the 21st Century by Robert Kiyosaki

Think and Grow Rich by Napoleon Hill

7 Strategies for Wealth & Happiness by Jim Rohn

How to Win Friends and Influence People by Dale Carnegie

Mach II With Your Hair on Fire by Richard Brooke

The Greatest Networker in the World by John Milton Fogg

The Power of Focus by Jack Canfield, Mark Victor Hansen, and Les Hewitt

The 45-Second Presentation that Will Change Your Life by Don Failla

The Greatest Salesman in the World by Og Mandino

The Psychology of Winning by Denis Waitley

Unlimited Power by Anthony Robbins

The book of *Proverbs* in *The Bible* (ancient teaching on money, business and people from King Solomon, the richest man who ever lived)